Connecting Civic Engagement and Social Innovation

Campus Compact is a national coalition of colleges and universities committed to the public purposes of higher education. Campus Compact publications focus on practical strategies for campuses to put civic education and community engagement into action. Please visit http://compact.org for more information.

Campus Compact

Connecting Civic Engagement and Social Innovation

Toward Higher Education's Democratic Promise

EDITED BY
AMANDA MOORE MCBRIDE
AND ERIC MLYN

Campus Compact

BOSTON, MASSACHUSETTS
Distributed by Stylus Publishing, LLC.

Published by Campus Compact
89 South Street, Suite 103
Boston, MA 02111

Library of Congress Cataloging-in-Publication Data

The CIP data for this book has been applied for.

13-digit ISBN: 978-1-945459-21-4 (cloth)
13-digit ISBN: 978-1-945459-22-1 (paperback)
13-digit ISBN: 978-1-945459-24-5 (library networkable e-edition)
13-digit ISBN: 978-1-945459-23-8 (consumer e-edition)

Printed in the United States of America

All first editions printed on acid-free paper
that meets the American National Standards Institute
Z39-48 Standard.

First Edition, 2020

Eric dedicates this book to the memory of his late wife, Judy Byck, who in her own way was committed every day to making the world a better place.

Amanda dedicates this book to the life of her father, Covie Ray Moore, who came to live with her during its writing, reminding her that her interest in innovation came from his persistent entrepreneurial spirit.

CONTENTS

TABLES AND FIGURES

TABLES

FIGURES

ACKNOWLEDGMENTS

This book comes out of what has been more than a decade-long friendship between the two of us. We first met at a professional conference on civic engagement and realized that we not only had similar interests in how we could move civic engagement in higher education forward but also both loved the Grateful Dead. That was the beginning of a collaboration that has been professionally and personally enriching for both of us. Indeed, what a long strange trip it has been.

From our initial meeting, when Amanda was running civic engagement programs at Washington University of St. Louis and Eric was leading DukeEngage along with other civic initiatives at Duke University, we have pursued our interests in global service-learning. We further collaborated in 2011 on the first meeting of what is now a broad organization on global service-learning that is holding its sixth summit in 2020. We also began musing about the lack of political or democratic thinking in the civic engagement movements in higher education and wrote some short pieces for academic audiences that urged broader approaches to teaching about social change.

This edited volume grew out of a concern that we had about the rise of social entrepreneurship and social innovation on our campuses. It struck us as an important movement, and we wanted to place it in the broader context of how we teach and talk about social change on our campuses. This led to a 2015 think tank on social innovation and civic engagement that brought together practitioners and scholars from these fields. The challenges and synergies identified by the participants convinced us that there was more to be said about these movements, and thus the idea for this book was born.

Eric stepped down from his administrative role at Duke University and plans to return to the classroom. Amanda took on the deanship of the School of Social Work at the University of Denver. We both remain keenly interested in what we see as fundamental issues about how institutions of higher education work to foster and strengthen democracy. We are so pleased that the contributors to this volume have directly addressed this issue and offer creative ideas for pursuing a democratic mission. Given the current threats to democracy in the United States, we can think of few issues that are more important for our leaders in higher education to address.

Eric

I would like to thank many colleagues at Duke University who listened to my rants and raves about the growth of the social innovation movement. Matt Nash taught me much about this field and welcomed me into the growing social innovation and entrepreneurship initiative at Duke. Other colleagues at Duke who helped with my thinking on this and welcomed conversations over coffee or lunch include Tony Brown, Robert Korstad, and David Malone. I am also grateful to Marina Kim of Ashoka U who invited me into the Ashoka community. Finally, I thank Gary Bennett, Sally Kornbluth, Peter Lange, and Steve Nowicki for encouraging this scholarship and providing the funding for a sabbatical, which allowed for the completion of this project. On that note, I am grateful to colleagues at the Tisch College for Civic Life at Tufts University, in particular Peter Levine and Alan Solomont, who welcomed me as a visiting scholar for the fall of 2019. They have provided a comfortable and stimulating environment in which to finish this project and to think and read.

Amanda

I would like to thank my prior colleagues at Washington University in St. Louis, including Michael Sherraden, former provost Holden Thorp, and former dean Eddie Lawlor. All saw innovation, entrepreneurship, and civic engagement as critical to the mission of higher education, and gave me opportunities to pursue their intersection through research and curricular innovation campus wide. Now at the University of Denver, I am grateful for Chancellor Emerita Rebecca Chopp's vision to advance social innovation for the public good through the founding of Project X-ITE and allowing me to help shape its trajectory. Kimberly Bender, Hope Wisneski, and Trish Becker at the Graduate School of Social Work; Nina Sharma and Marty Katz at Project X-ITE; and JB Holston shared the ride, becoming my thought partners and coconspirators on the disruption so badly needed in higher education.

PART ONE

INTRODUCTION

Chapter One

FRAMING THE ISSUES BETWEEN THE CIVIC ENGAGEMENT AND SOCIAL INNOVATION MOVEMENTS IN HIGHER EDUCATION

Eric Mlyn and Amanda Moore McBride

As we write the first chapter of this book, we ask ourselves, in the words of David Byrne, "Well, how did I get here?" (Talking Heads, 1980). Neither of us thought five years ago when we first published our critiques of the social innovation movement that we would be where we are now, which is right in the middle of the social innovation movements on our respective university campuses. We have moved from critics on the periphery to central players in our campuses' social innovation efforts. One of us is now a named cochangemaker at Duke University as a university liaison to Ashoka U, and one of us is now dean of a school of social work who is working across schools at the University of Denver to develop the innovation and entrepreneurship center for the university. As we have evolved, we have become acutely aware that so have these movements.

This book is about this evolution, where civic engagement and social innovation have been, where they are now, and where their potential lies. It has been an exciting time for those of us teaching, researching, and running programs in these areas; we welcome this opportunity to take a step back to make meaning of the field. To the extent that we always encourage our students to reflect on their experiences and learning, we welcome the opportunity to do that here with you the reader and our colleagues who have written provocative perspectives on these issues.

In working on this volume, it became evident to us that we need to be clear on the ultimate purpose of the civic engagement and social innovation movements. What are they trying to achieve? We contend that the unifier of these two approaches is betterment of the human condition, improving the social, economic, and political conditions for the majority. *Social change* is often the identified goal and phrase used. As civic engagement scholars, we struggle with this reference because our conception of social change is sometimes too narrowly focused on policy change, a conception with a premise that government may be best equipped to better the human condition at scale. However, we concede that most do use social change as the outcome measure and that we can achieve it in a myriad of ways. In light of this, we are eager to broaden our own conception of the wide variety of mechanisms that citizens use to better the human condition and the role that higher education plays in encouraging, pursuing, and teaching these mechanisms.

As a frame to this book and the contributors' chapters, we begin with the ongoing critiques of both approaches, and then our contributors address specific themes. In Part Two, this volume explores the historical and contemporary context of these approaches. In Part Three, the contexts are embedded in the paradigmatic anchor institution approach. In Part Four, the book offers ways to move the approaches forward. We discuss the democratic foundations (or absence thereof) of both approaches, elaborating on existing critiques and offering new ones. We conclude with possible future directions that may make the approaches more effective for fulfilling the broader democratic mission of U.S. higher education. All of this will outline the issues, not offer up definitive conclusions. We invite you to come to your own conclusions and test them against those we offer in the final chapter. Our hope is that those in higher education who wish to promote and advance social change will critically examine where we are with our civic engagement and social innovation approaches and commit to realizing their promise through changes in our operations and our educational processes, pedagogical strategies, evaluation metrics, and outcomes.[1]

Evolving Critiques

We maintain some degree of skepticism about the ascendance of the social innovation movement, but we also embrace an openness to its possibilities. Our aim is to be productive in moving the respective civic engagement and social innovation approaches forward. In editing this book, we have also been reminded that the more traditional civic engagement approaches we were raised on suffer from some of the very same critiques that we have leveled at social innovation. We deeply appreciate the wisdom of the profound and simple observation by Nobel Laureate Thomas Schelling (1966) that it is much easier to destroy something than to build it. In the end, the world simply has too many problems and unmet needs for us to pretend that we have a clear view or evidence on the single best approach for achieving social change and how higher education best educates toward that goal. We are grateful to those who have joined us in writing this book—at once being critical and constructive.

Some of our critiques of social innovation have been named previously and remain (McBride & Mlyn, 2015, 2016): Innovation is still much overused, ideas are still prized over execution, and self-confidence is weighted more than community wisdom. These critiques stem at least in part from the deluge of e-mails and talks and colloquia and webinars that seek to push the role of innovation to the forefront of everything we do. In an attempt to "disrupt" and change social conditions, social innovation can sometimes be a false promise, because we risk abandoning the other ways that democracies achieve social change, such as through organizing, voting, and protesting. There can be opportunity costs when our students and citizens more generally become enamored with social innovation while ignoring the politics of our time. As such, social innovation has been unapologetically apolitical, seeking the technical solution, when the social issues it attempts to affect are anything but technical or apolitical. But, and this volume represents an evolution of our thinking, civic engagement as traditionally pursued in higher education has also much of the time been apolitical and not particularly concerned with democracy. An example is that the primary mode of student civic engagement is through volunteering efforts, such as tutoring children or cleaning parks (Mlyn & McBride, 2014).

Those who have contributed to this volume have propelled our thinking on this point, such that we now think there are real possibilities to further develop the social innovation movement to more fully embrace the democratic virtues that are ultimately necessary for impactful and scalable social change. One area where this has become particularly clear to us over the last four years is in civic tech, where new organizations, websites, and apps reduce the transaction costs of democratic citizenship. Of note here are innovations such as TurboVote, Countable, and VoteWithMe; we are both impressed with the power of technology to enhance our democracy (Civictech, 2019). We will briefly return to these topics in the conclusion.

Still Needed: Clarification and Grounding

We have written previously on the need to define terms in this social change arena of higher education (McBride & Mlyn, 2016). It does not serve us to be sloppy and nondescript in our language and references, especially as we attempt to build a field. We recognize that definitions are important. Every chapter in this volume defines terms. We are also aware that one could dedicate an entire volume to the various definitions that we use in both civic engagement and social innovation, their historical evolution, and the important implications that result from these definitional choices. We are not going to do that important but enormous task here. Instead, for the purposes of bringing some commonality to our language in this chapter and throughout this volume, we offer this most commonly accepted frame of reference:

> Civic engagement means working to make a difference in the civic life of our communities and developing the combination of knowledge, skills, values and motivation to make that difference. It means promoting the quality of life in a community, through both political and non-political processes. (Ehrlich, 2000, p. vi)

Students can be involved in civic activities through higher education by volunteering, serving internationally, interning for politicians or political organizations, and so on.

The first editor's note of the leading journal *Stanford Social Innovation Review* defined *social innovation* as "the process of inventing, securing support for, and implementing novel solutions to social needs and problems" (Phills, Deiglmeier, & Miller, 2008, p. 36). Like social entrepreneurship, social innovation connotes the development and introduction of something new, but that new thing can be an idea, a device, or a process—not just an enterprise or an organization or a company. The innovation is "social" because it intends to address some pressing problem affecting the human condition. Students can be involved in social innovation efforts in a variety of ways, such as by taking courses, completing internships, working on team projects, participating in competitions, and engaging in a range of other activities.

With this framing of social innovation in mind, we are struck by the sometimes misleading or inappropriate uses of each of the terms. A metaphor about democracy is apt: One cannot help but notice the normative global appeal of the notion of *democracy* and use of the term even by regimes that do not resemble any of our notions of democracy. So, too, do many overstate the social benefits of businesses that were created solely to make a profit. Similarly, the normative appeal of social benefit leads to its evocation to justify massive profit-making companies, such as Airbnb and Uber. Those companies are first and foremost about making money and delivering value for their shareholders, though they often invoke the social benefits of their work, whether framed in terms of impact on the environment or wages. (Perhaps the trust test here is whether any of these companies of the so-called sharing economy would ever sacrifice financial revenue for these broader social causes.) Similarly, we hear things described as innovative that are not. One of us attended a conference some years ago where the creation of the "deconstructed lunch" was heralded as a remarkable innovation that would lessen the environmental impact of the conference. When described, the deconstructed lunch—sans boxes—was not much more than a buffet. The point here is not to be snarky, but instead to emphasize that notions of social innovation are so normatively appealing that they can be overused and verge on becoming meaningless.

We also have mused among ourselves and with other colleagues about why the field of social innovation is ascendant right now. It is clear that so many of today's entrepreneurs achieved their fame as innovators; here we are thinking of the likes of Steve Jobs, Bill Gates, Elon Musk, and Jeff Bezos, to name just a few. It is much harder for any of us to name figures from the public and nonprofit sectors who receive the same amount of adulation. In this age of rapid technological growth and innovations, which were simply hard to imagine only a few years ago, it is perhaps only logical that so many would think we can bring the same innovative genius to our attempts to solve hunger, homelessness, and violence. And to be fair, we recognize that many social innovations—from apps that connect excess food at events to populations that need the food to large-scale innovations, such as City Year or Teach for America—have had a real impact in making the world a better place. Of course, it also becomes obvious here that what is innovative at one point in history becomes the standard as time moves on.

As we reflect on our milieu of higher education, the ascendance of social innovation should be viewed as related to broader trends in higher education. The entire higher education industry—both public and private institutions—has embraced neoliberal, market-based strategies, which leaves an embrace of innovation and entrepreneurship as the logical next step for U.S. higher education. There have also been some fairly broad-based attacks on the general approach and logic of a liberal arts education, arguing that our institutions of higher education need to do a better job of adopting more instrumental approaches to educating students so that they are ready for the job market.

We join many other defenders of the liberal arts tradition by recognizing that the skills of critical analysis, problem-solving, and teamwork prepare our students for the workplace of the twenty-first century, even though there is pressure to give our students what many narrowly refer to as *real skills*, such as coding and financial literacy. As a result, education that focuses on creating entrepreneurs (whether social or not) is somehow seen as being more instrumental. This has allowed institutions with a liberal arts focus to educate for social innovation, thus tipping their hats to preparing students for the workforce, whatever that now means. Finally, we agree with David Scobey, who argues in this volume that the language of innovation and entrepreneurship speaks to many higher education donors as it embraces assumptions and vocabularies that are consistent with the business world from which many of them derive their wealth.

A Democratic Focus as the Next Frontier

Both civic engagement and social innovation are united in that neither currently emphasizes democracy. The political process is not the primary tool for social change. That said, there is a burgeoning societal awakening that we should embrace politics, the common good, and democracy in all its weaknesses. We join our colleagues in this volume in hitching the civic engagement and social innovation approaches to this call for democratic renewal. Our call for a new emphasis on democracy by these approaches is justified through empirical evidence that our students would rather volunteer than vote. This call takes on new urgency and resonance because of the current fundamental threats to democracy—things such as freedom of the press, the independence of the courts, and the sanctity of the rule of law. Although this call for democratic engagement is not new, it is now more important than ever.

What does higher education have to do with democracy? Almost all of our mission statements have some call to foster, educate, and train future citizens to bolster democracy and the betterment of society. The chapters that follow seek to reclaim that purpose by broadening and deepening both civic engagement and social innovation approaches and identifying the important areas of intersection. The primary methods that higher education has used to engage its students in efforts of social change have not emphasized democracy—whether those efforts are considered civic engagement or social innovation. You will see this point emerge in the following chapters, as will strategies for a more promising direction.

Note

1. We recognize here the pioneering work of Sandra Enos (2015) and her book *Service-Learning and Social Entrepreneurship in Higher Education: A Pedagogy of Social Change*. Enos's research and conclusions deeply inform our work and perspective, and the interviews she did with schools provide important empirical evidence for our consideration.

References

Civictech. (2019). Home. Retrieved from https://civictech.guide/

Ehrlich, T. (Ed.). (2000). *Civic responsibility and higher education*. Westport, CT: Oryx Press.

Enos, S. (2015). *Service-learning and social entrepreneurship in higher education: A pedagogy of social change*. New York, NY: Palgrave Macmillan.

McBride, A. M., & Mlyn, E. (2015, February 2). Innovation alone won't fix social problems. *The Chronicle of Higher Education*. Retrieved from https://www.chronicle.com/article/Innovation-Alone-Won-t-Fix/151551

McBride, A. M., & Mlyn, E. (2016). Social innovation and civic engagement in higher education: Toward a shared future? *Diversity & Democracy*, *19*(3), 1–7.

Mlyn, E., & McBride, A. M. (2014, February 27). Civic engagement and higher education: It is not only about tutoring. *Huffington Post*. Retrieved from https://www.huffpost.com/entry/civic-engagement-and-high_b_4860150

Phills, J., Jr., Deiglmeier, K., & Miller, D. (2008). Rediscovering social innovation. *Stanford Social Innovation Review, 6(4)*, 34–43.

Schelling, T. (1966). *Arms and influence*. New Haven, CT: Yale University Press.

Talking Heads. (1980). Once in a lifetime [song]. On *Remain in Light*. Sire Records.

PART TWO

HISTORY AND CONTEMPORARY CONTEXT

Chapter Two

SIBLING RIVALS OR KISSING COUSINS?

Community Engagement, Social Innovation, and Higher Education for the Public Good

David Scobey

When my academic career made a turn toward community work in the late 1990s, the movement for community engagement was already well established. Campus Compact was more than a decade old, drawing inspiration from even older traditions of campus-based service and student volunteerism. Service-learning courses, programs, and centers existed on hundreds of colleges and universities, among them my home institution at the time, the University of Michigan at Ann Arbor. But the movement was also going through a period of growth and change. There were wide-ranging efforts to enlarge its practice to include long-term community partnerships and public scholarship; there were wide-ranging efforts to extend its academic reach from the social sciences and helping professions across the liberal arts.

The Arts of Citizenship Program, which I founded at the University of Michigan in 1998, drew on and contributed to such developments. So did two new academic consortia on whose advisory boards I sat: Project Pericles (dedicated to citizenship education in liberal arts institutions) and Imagining America (dedicated to the role of the arts, humanities, and design in democratic public life). In 2005, I left Michigan to lead a new center for community partnerships at Bates College. Five years later,

I joined The New School in New York as dean of an experimental division committed to public engagement and practice-based learning. There I was fortunate to oversee the exemplary Social Innovation Initiative and to educate myself about the emergent movement for social entrepreneurship and social innovation on American campuses. For two decades, I have been a partisan of the civic turn in higher education—and more recently, a cheerleader for the innovation turn.

My point in starting with these autobiographical scraps is not to offer my credentials for writing this essay. Rather I want to make clear why I take its theme—the relationship between community engagement and social innovation—so seriously. My own experience underscores the complexity of that relationship. These movements seem to me at once resonant with and different from one another in their educational practices, the values that animate those practices, and the historical and institutional contexts where those values and practices were forged. There is both common ground and creative tension, both historical continuity and generational disjuncture between them. And that play of resonance and dissonance seems to me a good thing. For it reminds us that there is no single, correct, totalizing way to commit higher education to the public good. Varying frameworks will define and enact that commitment according to their own lights, informed by their distinctive values, practices, and genealogies.

My aim here is to place these similar but different movements in dialogue with one another. I do so in the belief that such dialogue will illuminate the strengths and limitations of each—and the belief that it can make each of them stronger and *less* limited. It can suggest settings and projects where the integration of community engagement and social innovation will prove mutually generative as well as other situations where each practice might fruitfully go its own way. Perhaps most importantly, it can point to new opportunities for work within each movement and between them. For that is the other thing my personal journey has taught me: The relationship between community engagement and social innovation—and the democratic project to which both contribute—remains unfinished.

The Public Good Tradition

Let's start by noting that the two movements share a core set of values and a historical relationship. Indeed, they share a core set of values *because* they have a historical relationship. They are chapters in a longer, larger tradition of higher education for the public good, a tradition that has been variously committed to expanding educational opportunity, serving community needs, bringing the gifts of the academy to bear on social problems, strengthening democratic citizenship—and (in the process) offering a more vibrant education to more students. This public-good tradition has a rich and wide-ranging history in the United States. It includes land-grant universities and community colleges, historically black institutions and women's colleges, and labor education programs like the Bryn Mawr Summer School and radical pedagogy experiments like Antioch College. As such examples underscore, it has often centered on democratizing access for nonelite, nonwhite, and nonmale undergraduates; some of its most storied victories involve the founding of new institutions to do just that.[1]

The recent surge of interest in community engagement and social innovation reflects a different emphasis: the forging of new educational practices *within* academic institutions that meld experiential learning with social engagement. These movements have been pedagogically creative in ways that are strikingly resonant with one another. Both have evolved models of project-based work and active, collaborative, interdisciplinary learning aimed at taking on *wicked problems*. Both have done so by challenging the atomistic, flattening effects of traditional academic practices, such as the semester form, the credit-hour economy, and the specialized disciplinary curriculum. Indeed, both challenge the boundaries between the curriculum and the cocurriculum, between term time and off time, and between academic space (campus, classroom, lab) and the larger world. And unlike, for example, employment internships, both social innovation and civic engagement pursue this type of engaged, experiential learning in order to leverage academic resources for social benefit.

Yet, given all these commonalities, the differences are also striking. The movements for community engagement and social innovation emerged out of disparate regions of the academy. Their practices were shaped by disparate influences, both within and without higher education. They differ in the ways they construe the larger social worlds in which they work. And they differ in the ways they aim to educate and empower students to do that work. A closer look at the histories of the two movements—their origins and development within the public-good tradition—can illuminate both the resonances and dissonances between them.

Genealogies of Community Engagement

The community engagement movement is the older of the two, and its institutional genealogy is rooted, as I have noted, in the social sciences and in helping professions, such as public health and social work. To be more precise, it emerged as an internal rebellion *within* the social sciences and the helping professions *against* their dominant paradigms of positivistic research and technical expertise. Beginning in the 1960s and 1970s, that intellectual rebellion took various forms in various fields, inflected by a wide range of critical and contrarian voices: C. Wright Mills (1956, 1959) in sociology, Barrington Moore (1966) in political science, Paulo Freire (1970) in education, and Paul Farmer in public health (Kidder, 2003), to cite only a few. But a common response across many disciplines was the development of counternormative modes of pedagogy and research: service-learning (Kenny & Gallagher, 2002; Saltmarsh & Hartley, 2017), community-based or participatory action research (Wallerstein & Duran, 2008), and more broadly the scholarship of engagement (Boyer, 1996). These innovative practices were catalyzed by student and faculty activists within the academy, critical of its cult of technique and disciplinary expertise and its disengagement from—if not collusion with—larger social crises of racism, militarism, and poverty (Hollander, Lapping, Rice, & Cruz, 2017; Stanton, Giles, & Cruz, 1999). And they were catalyzed by traditions of popular education and social activism *outside* the academy, most notably the settlement house (Deegan, 2017; Roth, 2014), civil rights (Charron, 2009; Countryman & Eatman, 2017), and community-organizing movements (Boyte, 2004; Boyte & Kari, 1996; Horton, Kohl, & Kohl, 1998).

Informed by these larger currents, two initiatives were launched in the mid-1980s—one by college students, one by university leaders—that proved foundational to the community engagement movement. In 1984, two Harvard undergraduates, Wayne Meisel and Bobby Hackett, organized the Campus Outreach Opportunity League (COOL), a network of student advocates for service and social action on hundreds of campuses. During its 20-year tenure, COOL's yearly conferences became a crucial forum for student-led community engagement (IMPACT National Conference, n.d.; Saltmarsh & Hartley, 2017). (Meisel and Hackett went on to lead the Bonner Foundation, funding a network of community-service fellowship programs for low-income students on more than 50 campuses [The Corella & Bertram F. Bonner Foundation, n.d.].) In 1985, a year after the launch of COOL, the presidents of Brown University, Georgetown University, Stanford University, and the Education Commission of the States founded Campus Compact, an institutional consortium aimed at renewing the commitment of higher education to civic engagement and public service. Their call was timely: In the face of widespread concern about the disengagement of both college students and academic institutions—as well as growing anxiety about the fragmentation and devolution of American public life—Campus Compact grew with impressive urgency. Within a year, more than 100 institutions had joined the consortium; by 2002 it boasted more than 900 members, with some 20,000 faculty teaching service-learning courses (Campus Compact, 2002; Saltmarsh & Hartley, 2017).

If Campus Compact was the loudest voice for community engagement, it was by no means the only voice. Beginning in the late 1990s, the movement underwent a period of remarkable associational expansion (Saltmarsh & Hartley, 2017). Along with Meisel and Hackett's Bonner Network (started in 1990), there was Campus-Community Partnerships for Health, which was established in 1997 to advance equity and community collaboration in the health disciplines. The Imagining America consortium, dedicated to public work through the arts, humanities, and design, was launched a year later, and Project Pericles, a group of liberal arts institutions committed to civic engagement, was launched a year after that. In 2003, the American Association of State Colleges and Universities began the American Democracy Project, with some 250 participating campuses; a sibling initiative for community colleges, The Democracy Commitment, was started in 2011. Along with this organizational growth, a series of major reports and manifestos announced commitments to publicly engaged education in various sectors and associations: the *Wingspread Declaration on Renewing the Civic Mission of the American Research University* (Boyte & Hollander, 1999), *Returning to Our Roots: The Engaged Institution* (Kellogg Commission on the Future of State and Land-Grant Universities, 1999), *Stepping Forward as Stewards of Place: A Guide for Leading Public Engagement at State Colleges and Universities* (American Association of State Colleges and Universities, 2002), *Scholarship in Public: Knowledge Creation and Tenure Policy in the Engaged University* (Ellison & Eatman, 2008), and *A Crucible Moment: College Learning and Democracy's Future* (National Task Force on Civic Learning and Democratic Engagement, 2012, commissioned by the U.S. Department of Education and issued by the Association of American Colleges & Universities). Scholarship about community engagement flourished as well. In 1994, the *Michigan Journal of Community Service Learning* began publication, and 3 years later, the American Association of Higher Education launched *Service-Learning in the Disciplines*, publishing more than 20 field-specific monographs under the editorial leadership of Edward Zlotkowski.

During the 1990s and mid-2000s, in short, community-based teaching, research, and project work had taken root in every discipline and sector of the academy. This was, as I have noted, the period when my own career turned to public engagement. What I experienced was not just the gravitational pull of aggregative growth. A true community of practice had come together, within which practitioners, advocates, and scholars like me could iteratively develop, critique, and improve our work. Its spirit was both bracing and embracing, collaborative and argumentative. Nadinne Cruz and George Sanchez (among others) challenged what they saw as the colonialist implications of a service-learning model that posited white, middle-class college students going "out there" to benefit working-class communities of color (Hollander et al., 2017; Sanchez, 2004). John Saltmarsh, Matt Hartley, and Patti Clayton (among others) challenged what they saw as a depoliticized model of civic rather than democratic engagement (Saltmarsh, Hartley, & Clayton, 2009). Many faculty and staff—myself among them—critiqued the category of service itself for its apparent tacit assumption of noblesse oblige and its deficit notions of the communities where we worked.

Yet out of the convenings, critiques, experiments, and arguments, a new through-line emerged, a rough consensus about the movement's values and best practice (Scobey, 2011, 2014b). What began in the 1980s and 1990s with the platform of the stand-alone service-learning course evolved into a new model of long-term, sustained partnerships. It stressed a commitment to not only students' experiential learning but also community-based teaching, publicly engaged research, and institutional citizenship. It was grounded in an ethos of reciprocity and dialogue, of collaboration *with* communities rather than service *to* them. At its best, such collaboration would enable students to link their cognitive, civic, and personal development; faculty to link their teaching, research, and community commitments; and communities to pursue both concrete benefits and longer term capacity building and sociopolitical change. Or so we hoped.

Genealogies of Social Innovation

My personal trajectory led me eventually to The New School, where, as dean of a division dedicated to public engagement, I helped to oversee the new (and for me utterly novel) Social Innovation Initiative. In retrospect, it is not surprising that I knew so little about such work. Although I felt at once its resonance with my community engagement world, the movement for social innovation was rooted in a different academic geography and intellectual genealogy. It emerged largely from business schools and the design and engineering professions. Or, to be more precise, it emerged—just like the movement for community engagement—as an internal critique. The turn to social innovation was a reaction against the dominance of technocratic and neoliberal assumptions within the fields of management, engineering, planning, and policy studies—assumptions that too often divorced technical and economic efficiencies from ethical values and human needs.

The intellectual history of this countertradition has yet to be fully fleshed out, perhaps because it is still relatively young. Yet (again like community engagement) it had taproots both inside and outside higher education. Donald Schon's (1983) *The Reflective Practitioner: How Professionals Think in Action* seems to me a general influence, with its powerful call to shift professional education away from technical mastery and toward the cultivation of reflection, craft-like judgment, and open-ended problem-solving. More specifically, however, the practices and programs of the social innovation movement were developed in two disciplinary spaces. In the 1990s, business faculty began to forge a new subfield of "social entrepreneurship" at elite universities, such as Harvard, Stanford, Yale, and Duke (Worsham, 2012). "The time is certainly ripe for entrepreneurial approaches to social problems," argued one of its pioneers, Greg Dees, in a 2001 essay. "Many governmental and philanthropic efforts have fallen far short of our expectations. Major social sector institutions are often viewed as inefficient, ineffective, and unresponsive. Social entrepreneurs are needed to develop new models for a new century" (Dees, 2001, p. 1). A decade later, *Harvard Business Review* reported that social entrepreneurship and the "double bottom-line" were being taught in hundreds of management courses and cases (Milway & Goulay, 2013). At just the same time, David Kelley and his colleagues on the Stanford engineering faculty launched the Hasso Plattner Institute of Design (founded in 2008)—colloquially known as the Stanford d.school—as a kind of heterodox studio for teaching creativity and design-based problem-solving (Kelley & Kelley, 2013).

These curricular beachheads were themselves shaped by influences beyond the academy. Stanford's Kelley was a principal of IDEO, the famed studio whose product-development and consulting practice spread the gospel of human-centered design and creative innovation as underused approaches to social betterment (Brown, 2009; Kelley & Kelley, 2013).[2] Even more important was Bill Drayton, the founder of Ashoka: Innovators for the Public. In the aftermath of the Reagan Revolution—and having already worked in both government and management consulting—Drayton called for new models of policy-making and social action grounded in the creative energies of grassroots changemakers. Such innovators, he argued, would develop and disseminate citizen-sector, so-called third-way interventions that transcended the stale binaries of market individualism and technocratic regulation. Animated by a belief in the democratic abundance of social creativity—"everyone a changemaker" is the rallying cry—Ashoka has served as a global network, funding infrastructure, mentoring space, and community of practice for social innovation work (Ashoka, n.d.; Ashoka U., n.d.).

As with the community engagement movement, this mix of intramural and external influences sparked the development of associational networks and consortia across higher education. In 2007, the Clinton Global Initiative started CGI University to support "a growing community of young leaders who don't just discuss global challenges," but "take real, concrete steps toward solving them" (CGI U, n.d.b). The following year saw the launch of Ashoka U, a consortium of Changemaker Campuses whose mission is "to make social innovation and changemaking the new norm in higher education and beyond" (Ashoka U, n.d.). Both groups boast dozens of member campuses, and their annual convenings serve as venues for sharing work, distilling models, and organizing. They compose in effect the networked infrastructure of the academic social innovation movement, its functional equivalent to Campus Compact, COOL, and Imagining America.

Here, however, the themes and practices are different. Whereas my colleagues and I focused on—and argued about—the shape of community-based courses, the value of public scholarship, and the ethics of project partnerships, the social innovation movement has stressed the mentoring and empowerment of students as changemakers and the support of student-led interventions and social enterprises. At CGI U's annual meetings, for instance, hundreds of participants offer "Commitments to Action": discrete, generally self-contained projects that "address a specific challenge with a defined course of action and detailed objectives," with "results that are measurable and can be reported back to CGI U" (CGI U, n.d.a). The New School's Social Innovation Initiative has a similar focus: It features an annual "New Challenge" in which student teams develop social-action projects with the guidance of faculty and community mentors, competing to win awards of up to $10,000 to implement their proposals over several years (Kahane, 2016).

This focus on student changemaking is by no means static. Social innovation educators have used their networks and convenings to foster experimentation and critique, testing and evolving their vocabulary, values, and models (Kim, 2015; Kim & Krampetz, 2016). Just as community-engaged academics debated the implications of service and partnership, shifting our work away from the paternalistic implications of the former, so too the younger movement has debated the implications of social entrepreneurship and social innovation, shifting increasingly away from the business-oriented implications of the former. Just as community-based research and teaching expanded their scope beyond the social sciences and helping professions, so too have social innovation educators reached beyond the fields of business, design, and engineering. The New School's student competition, for instance, elicits hundreds of proposals from not only design and policy teams but also students in the university's media, performance, and liberal arts programs (Kahane, 2016). At its best, argue the movement's adherents, such a capacious vision can make every *student* a changemaker—and make the academy itself an exemplar of creative innovation and social betterment. Or so they hope.

Counterpoints

This thumbnail history suggests a complex mix of likeness and difference between the two movements. Their developmental paths have been remarkably similar, like twins born 15 years apart. Both emerged in opposition to dominant traditions in their home disciplines. Both were catalyzed by intellectual and political influences within and outside the academy. Both created counternormative practices that melded teaching and learning with social action. Both distilled and disseminated these practices in new consortia and associational networks, using the distributed geography of higher education to convene communities of practice to test, critique, and improve their work. And yet their academic lineages and homelands, their core practices and discourses, are utterly different. Their institutional disconnection and intellectual distance from one another are as striking as their developmental similarities. If they are twins at all, they are certainly not identical.

Nowhere are the differences more salient than in the ways the two movements view their public mission and construe the social world in which they pursue it. The innovation framework tends to cast the social world as a landscape of problems, a landscape that needs above all problem-*solvers*. On such a view, the world is not simply unfair, unequal, and unjust; it is also stuck. It requires the intervention of changemakers—armed with new technologies, new market incentives, new policy levers—who pursue the public good by unmiring it. I do not mean to imply that this framework is technocratic or instrumental. Quite the opposite: Social innovation activists are deeply committed to human-centered design. They increasingly critique their initial paradigm of the individualist entrepreneur-hero in favor of more collaborative, horizontal, grassroots models of action: "*Everyone* a changemaker" (Ashoka, n.d.). Nonetheless the movement remains dedicated, at base, to a practice of intervention *in* the world, a practice whose gold standard is measurable social betterment brought about by innovative action (Kim, 2015; Kim & Krampetz, 2016).

By contrast, it seems to me that the community engagement framework tends to view the world as a landscape of *relationships*—relationships that need to be actively, ongoingly cocreated in a society where we are divided by both difference and inequality. Cocreation *with* community, rather than problem-solving *for* the community, is the mantra of the movement. As I have noted, this commitment to reciprocity and collaboration was the product of self-critique, of unease with the movement's initial focus on "service," with the dangers of noblesse oblige, with the arrogance of assuming a standpoint of professional authority or charitable condescension toward community partners. For 20 years, engaged academics like me have argued that viewing the social world as a landscape of problems on which to bestow solutions tends to ignore the assets of communities, to marginalize their voices, to misrecognize their problems, and to produce less benefit. Our atom of work became not the community project itself but rather the relationship with community partners by which problems are collaboratively named and projects cocreated.

Moreover, in construing the larger society so differently, the two frameworks view students differently as well. The community engagement movement, with its emphasis on mutuality and sustained partnerships, tends to treat students as civic apprentices in a larger world of stakeholders and issues, a world that requires time and patience to understand. As a result, students are often enlisted into ongoing projects not of their own devising. As a director of a center for community partnerships at Bates College, for instance, I partnered with a local history museum to research and create a traveling exhibition, "Weaving a World," about the experience of textile millworkers in Lewiston, Maine, Bates's (deindustrialized) hometown. The former leader of Museum L-A, Rachel Desgrosseilliers, and I conceived the scope and the goals of the project together. Successive teams of students in my public-history classes and during two summers did extraordinary archival research, oral history interviews, and thematic planning. They were true collaborators in the making of a significant public cultural resource. But they did not have the agency to define the project from the ground up. Indeed, I would argue "Weaving a World" proved educationally transformative for them precisely because—as in the rest of life—they had to plunge into a public sphere and contribute to a set of public needs not of their own making.[3]

By contrast, as I have said, the empowerment of students as self-active changemakers is the very heart of social innovation pedagogy. This is why grant or pitch competitions are so ubiquitous; they are a powerful means of igniting and channeling students' energy, creativity, and hunger to make a difference. The results can be impressive, even inspiring, as The New School's annual competition made clear to me. Examples of the New Challenge winners include "STEAM Punk" (maker kits designed for young people in Kabul, Afghanistan, to explore technology and design), "Drive Change" (a plan to use food trucks to offer formerly incarcerated youth job training and employment), and "Project Fogg" (a communications kit for communities to use in the immediate aftermath of a disaster) (Kahane, 2016). Such proposals underscore the power of the social innovation model to catalyze students' creativity and boldness. It tends to foster a kind of quick-strike interventionism that uses the fuel of their passion to drive their learning and social imagination. Conversely it tends *not* to foster an extended immersion in the problems they aim to solve or the communities they aim to benefit. We might say that the pedagogy of social innovation teaches students the social value of chutzpah, while that of community engagement stresses the social value of humility.

These differences—results versus relationships, students as apprentice citizens versus students as daring entrepreneurs—tend also to produce different scales and speeds of public work. As The New School projects suggest, social innovation pedagogy generally yields shorter, more compact interventions, often "pop-up" resources meant to disrupt and reorient our sense of possibilities. They are designed as action-forcing events for people whose situations are stuck in convention or dysfunction. Students are drawn to such work, in my experience, out of a wonderful desire to make something immediate and effective, a kind of "killer app" for social change; and that desire for efficacy can make them impatient with the more iterative change-work that community partnerships aim to achieve.

By contrast, projects like "Weaving a World," the Lewiston public-history exhibition, tend to be slow cooked, unfolding over several years in a series of phases. Key insights and strategies emerge via intermediate products, midcourse corrections, and ongoing dialogue (Scobey, 2014). Moreover, because the work is grounded in a partnership that will continue beyond the initial project, it can generate further ventures. After "Weaving a World" was shuttered, for instance, faculty, staff, and students at Bates College helped to curate new exhibitions with Museum L-A. They served as docents and board members. And the students who took part could—if they chose—work iteratively with the museum throughout their college career, from courses to volunteering to summer internships to community-based research to capstone projects ("Museum L-A Partnership," n.d.). Such a pedagogical model may not feed the students' hunger to make change *now*. But it does feed a different hunger: for an education that integrates students into larger life-worlds and integrates their learning experiences into a holistic, unfolding arc.

Cross-Pollination

Let's not overdraw these differences between community engagement education and social innovation education. They don't amount to a zero-sum conflict so much as they are disparate tendencies within a shared commitment to education for the public good. And it is important to remember that neither movement has been set in its ways. As I have stressed, both are notable for their internal dynamism; their penchant for experimentation; their openness to self-criticism; and their willingness to debate and revise core values, vocabulary, and practices. So it is not surprising that they have started to lean toward and engage one another. More and more their practitioners are represented at each other's convenings; on many campuses, their programs are colocated. And as this volume shows, they—we—are starting to think, write, and work together. It is precisely at such a moment that we need to place the two movements in dialogue, encouraging them to interrogate, challenge, and learn from each other in a spirit of critical generosity.

Many community engagement practitioners (if you cornered us in a quiet moment) would confess to a touch of envy and a great deal of admiration for the social innovation phenomenon. The envy perhaps reflects the attitude of a middle-aged movement, whose development has plateaued a bit, toward the high metabolism and continuing growth of its younger counterpart. (Truth be told, it may also reflect the feeling that social innovation programs have had an easier time winning support from donors and deans who are drawn more to the discourse of entrepreneurship than to that of citizenship.) Our bigger response—admiration—is for the intensity of excitement and engagement that the social innovation approach elicits in students. The hundreds of participants who attend CGI U and Ashoka U meetings, who craft proposals for pitch competitions, make clear how deeply the movement sparks their imagination. I am especially impressed by the skill with which social innovation pedagogy integrates student leadership development, a commitment to social change, experiential learning, and design thinking.

All of which pose as friendly challenges to my own movement's models of pedagogy and community collaboration. Too often, it seems to me, we have underestimated students' capacity for self-agency. Too often, we have appealed exclusively to their earnest idealism without also engaging their playfulness and creative imagination. Despite our movement's (rightful) allergy to noblesse oblige, to deficit models of community, and to the cult of heroic expertise, I believe we can learn from social entrepreneurs that nothing strengthens community trust and student engagement better than action and measurable impacts.

At the same time, it would be fruitful for social innovation educators and practitioners to learn from our paradigm of sustained collaborative work in and with communities. Academic institutions have a long history of helicopter interventions. Our community partners rightly ask us to demonstrate our staying power, our follow-through, our capacity for deep and active listening, long after the design prototyping is done and the students are gone. Otherwise those communities would tire of working with us. Nowhere is this challenge clearer than in the problem of the failed project. For student innovators, we know, failure can be generative; they cannot grow as changemakers without it. Yet for the community partner, failure is corrosive. It threatens trust; it thins out resources of energy and hope that are often scarce in underserved communities. Social innovation programs need to develop practices that can navigate between the valuable risk-taking of student chutzpah and the careful sustaining of bonds with the communities they seek to benefit.

We need, of course, the virtues of both approaches. We need to nurture both chutzpah *and* humility. We need results *and* relationships. We need killer interventions for social change *and* long-term, grounded shifts in community well-being and power. We need pedagogies and projects that can embody both the horizontal ethics of collaboration *and* the diagonal gifts of outside-the-box design thinking. And we need exemplars whose public work demonstrates what can happen when these frameworks converge. Fortunately, we have some.

The Work of Convergence

A might be the best-known social entrepreneur in the world: Muhammad Yunus. An economist by training, Yunus is justly celebrated for developing the practice of microlending as an antipoverty strategy and for institutionalizing it in the Grameen Bank, launched in his native Bangladesh in 1983. Microlending is strikingly straightforward, compact, and fairly easy to replicate; it seeks to dislodge poor entrepreneurs (especially female entrepreneurs) from penury by providing tiny amounts of capital to borrowers whose lack of income and collateral excludes them from the conventional banking economy (Yunus, 1999). Measured in repayment rates, individual upward mobility, and community development, the practice has shown significant results (Goldberg, 2005). Although its systemic effectiveness in reducing poverty remains widely debated (Banerjee, Karlan, & Zinman, 2015; Schiller, 2015). What is not debatable is the transformative impact of the practice on antipoverty policy and strategy. Development banks, aid agencies, and philanthropic foundations—particularly Yunus's own Grameen Foundation, founded in 1997—have adapted microfinance throughout the world. Yunus himself received the Nobel Peace Prize for it in 2006.

In his autobiography, *Banker to the Poor*, Yunus (1999) recounts how he evolved the practice. It was a response to his own experience of helplessness in the face of the poverty and famine afflicting Bangladesh in the 1970s and 1980s—and his frustration at both the disengagement of capitalists and the ineffectuality of government policy-makers. Microfinance was a third-way intervention par excellence, an alternative to the failures of neoliberalism and the failures of statist technocracy. Small wonder that Yunus is hailed alongside Bill Drayton as a founding hero of the social entrepreneurship movement; he was selected as one of the inaugural members of Ashoka's Global Academy for Social Entrepreneurship.

What is less known (unless you have read the whole account in *Banker to the Poor*) is how deeply Yunus's breakthrough depended on patient, grounded community engagement. The idea for microfinance germinated when—as a young economics professor at nearby Chittagong University—he began hanging out in the village of Jobra, looking for ways to counter his frustration with the failures of antipoverty policy through everyday, person-to-person work (Yunus, 1999). He befriended poor bamboo traders, mainly women, seeking to understand their entrapment in debt and poverty. "I was trying to see the problem from Sufia's point of view," he writes of one villager:

> I imagined I was a worm and had to overcome the obstacle facing me: how does one get around the cost of the bamboo? . . . I had no solution to Sufia's problem. I simply tried to understand why she suffered: she suffered because the cost of the bamboo was 5 *taka* and she didn't have the necessary cash. . . . Put in those terms it was simple. All I had to do was to lend her 5 *taka*. (Yunus, 1999, p. 10)

Everything that followed has become legend: Yunus's intuition about the usefulness of microcredits, the rebuffs he encountered from Bangladeshi banks and the United Nations, his decision to quit economics and become a "banker to the poor," the astonishing success of the new venture. But the legend of the heroic social entrepreneur obscures a paradox; as he himself insists, the chutzpah was grounded in humility: "I imagined I was a worm.... I had no solution to Sufia's problem" (p. 10). If Yunus's breakthrough technique entailed financial innovation, his process and purpose were grounded in a commitment to democratic agency—a commitment to not only inclusive, collaborative problem-solving but also a radical redistribution of power and voice. "Enable the poor, especially women," reads the mission statement of the Grameen Foundation, "to create a world without hunger and poverty" (Grameen Foundation, n.d.).

All of which is deeply resonant with a second exemplar: Exhibit B is the work of Caroline Wang and Mary Ann Burris, creators of the participatory photographic practice known as photovoice. In 1992, Wang (then a doctoral student in public health) and Burris (then a program officer in the Ford Foundation's Beijing office) were researching rural women's health needs, especially their reproductive health needs, in China's Yunnan province. Influenced by Freirian theories of popular education, by feminist critiques of gender hierarchy in social science research, and by the social documentary movement—Wang had studied documentary photography in college—they began to provide cameras to village women, asking them to pictorially express their community's social life, needs, and hopes. The photographs were developed, discussed by the participants in monthly meetings, and eventually presented to Chinese officials (Brown, 2015; Wang & Burris, 1997).

Beneath the simplicity of the practice—give cameras to community members—lay a nexus of ideas expressed in the term *photovoice* itself. Like Yunus, Wang and Burris aimed to amplify the voice and agency of marginalized communities, of the most marginalized members within those communities, in defining their own needs and devising their own proposals to governmental, policy, and academic experts. Unlike Yunus, however, they stressed the power of representation itself in this democratization of problem-solving and policy-making. It was essential to their work that the means of representation—the camera, the curating of its products—be as participatory and publicly shared as the discussion of community issues (Wang & Burris, 1997).

Like microfinance, photovoice proved replicable in many settings. It has been deployed in participatory-action research to address not only public health concerns but also youth development, homelessness, and many other community issues (Brown, 2015; Wang, Cash, & Powers, 2000). It is widely taught by faculty in anthropology, social work, and the visual arts. When (during my stint at Bates College) a local consortium of academic institutions opened a storefront education center in Lewiston, Maine, we commemorated the launch with a photographic exhibition shot and curated by downtown residents ("DEC: Downtown Education Collaborative," n.d.).

Photovoice is, in short, something of a poster child for the community engagement framework. It is grounded in the radical, participatory countertraditions of the social sciences and helping professions. It is not only trenchant in its critique of traditional hierarchies of expertise but also generative in using the shared authority of academic-community collaboration to produce new knowledge, new perspectives, and new interventions. In much the same way that the Grameen Bank has been an icon of the power of social innovation, photovoice exemplifies the sources and strengths of the community engagement movement. And, yet, here again there is a paradox, for the collaborative, bottom-up practice devised by Wang and Burris was also in its own way an example of compact, action-forcing interventionism. If microfinance demonstrated that chutzpah could be grounded in humility, photovoice showed something like the converse: that community engagement could be advanced through a practice of creative daring that inserted new technical capacities into the community.

These exemplars, in short, point to the possibilities of convergence between our two frameworks. Their work is simultaneously humble and bold, patient and impatient, democratic and entrepreneurial. They have been bracingly interventionist in critiquing and challenging powerful institutions, policies, and regimes of knowledge. Yet each began by listening to underserved communities—especially poor women in underserved communities—and the practices they devised were designed to enhance power and agency in those communities.

What would higher education look like at this point of convergence? How can the public-good tradition meld the strengths of both movements? These questions demand sustained dialogue and collaborative work on the part of social innovation and community engagement educators. I will not offer a full answer here. But I hope (perhaps betraying my own background and biases) that the sweet spot will not overemphasize the quick-strike interventionism of some current social innovation models. I would argue for maintaining the commitment to sustained partnerships that anchors the community engagement movement: partnerships that are slow cooked in trust building, listening, and dialogue. At the same time, however, I would want such partnerships to be open to—and eager for—an ethos of experimentation that will sometimes challenge both academic and community traditions. Such an educational model would be jazz-like in its multiple rhythms; it would commit academic institutions to both the ongoing beat and bass-line of civic connection and the improvisational riffing of social innovation. It would teach the value of both breakthrough and follow-through.

Let me hasten to add: Not every service-learning course or innovation lab or action research project should have to embody this holistic, all-encompassing ideal. Sometimes short-term, pop-up challenges are exactly what students need in order to grow and exactly what communities need in order to shake up their thinking. Sometimes the twentieth year of a community partnership, in which students are placed in schools or social service agencies or local museums, is just what sustains the community organization or alters that next student's journey forever. Yet in the long run, the public-good tradition in higher education requires more than pitch competitions and service placements. Even as these movements continue to evolve their distinctive goals and practices, we need them to learn and poach from one another, to collaborate, contend, and combine.

This work has already begun. Many civic engagement centers—for instance, Brown's Howard R. Swearer Center or Swarthmore's Lang Center—support robust social innovation initiatives. Design labs such as Auburn's celebrated Rural Studio already pursue long-term community collaboration. Meetings of Campus Compact and Ashoka U regularly include practitioners, researchers, and critics from "the other camp." And of course there are publications like this book. It is out of such cross-pollination and cross-training that the next, still-unimagined Grameen Bank or photovoice will emerge.

But if the work of convergence has begun, it has only just begun. It is time to take the relationship between community engagement and social innovation to another level, past metaphors of sibling rivals or kissing cousins or even cross-pollinators. It is time to forge communities of practice—within, without, and across academic institutions—that can incorporate and yet move beyond the particular strengths, limitations, and histories of each movement. What might such communities create? Perhaps new pedagogies and curricular structures in which projects, labs and seminars, long-term partnerships and short-form intensives are organically interwoven. Perhaps new organizational practices that enable colleges and universities to be both nimble laboratories of innovation and institutional citizens grounded in their communities. Perhaps something larger and longer: A new chapter in the history of higher education for the public good and the unfinished work of democratic renewal. Or so I hope.

Notes

1. I discuss the history of the public-good tradition in Scobey (2014a, 2017). There is rich scholarship on many aspects of the tradition—for instance, women's colleges, historically black institutions, land-grant universities, and the GI Bill—but a full, synthetic history remains to be written. It is also important to note that other countries, with their own educational histories, have quite different traditions of academic public engagement.

2. My own understanding of the pedagogical potential of design thinking owes much to working with Annette Diefenthaler, a talented, experienced designer in IDEO's education practice.

3. For a detailed account of the "Weaving a World" exhibition and the partnership between Bates College and Museum L-A, see Scobey (2014b). The exhibition panels and further materials are available at http://www.davidscobey.net/weaving-a-world.

References

American Association of State Colleges and Universities. (2002). *Stepping forward as stewards of place: A guide for leading public engagement at state colleges and universities.* Washington, DC: Author.

Ashoka. (n.d.). *About.* Retrieved from https://www.ashoka.org/en/about-ashoka

Ashoka U. (n.d.). *Changemaker campus.* Retrieved from http://ashokau.org/changemakercampus/

Banerjee, A., Karlan, D., & Zinman, J. (2015). Six randomized evaluations of microcredit: Introduction and further steps. *American Economic Journal: Applied Economics, 7*(1), 1–21.

Boyer, E. L. (1996). The scholarship of engagement. *Bulletin of the American Academy of Arts and Sciences, 49*(7), 18–33.

Boyte, H. (2004). *Everyday politics: Reconnecting citizens and public life.* Philadelphia, PA: University of Pennsylvania Press.

Boyte, H. C., & Hollander, E. (1999). *Wingspread declaration on renewing the civic mission of the American research university.* Providence, RI: Campus Compact.

Boyte, H., & Kari, N. N. (1996). *Building America: The democratic promise of public work.* Philadelphia, PA: Temple University Press.

Brown, A. (2015, May 21). *Photography & participation: How photovoice engages and rebuilds communities.* Retrieved from http://springboardexchange.org/photovoice/

Brown, T. (2009). *Change by design: How design thinking transforms organizations and inspires innovation.* New York, NY: HarperCollins.

Campus Compact. (2002). *2002 service statistics: Highlights of Campus Compact's annual membership survey.* Boston, MA: Author.

CGI U. (n.d.a). *About CGI U.* Retrieved from https://www.clintonfoundation.org/clinton-global-initiative/meetings/cgi-university/about/about-cgiu

CGI U. (n.d.b). *Commitment to action.* Retrieved from https://www.clintonfoundation.org/clinton-global-initiative/meetings/cgi-university/commitments/about-cgiu-commitments

Charron, K. M. (2009). *Freedom's teacher: The life of Septima Clark.* Chapel Hill, NC: University of North Carolina Press.

The Corella & Bertram F. Bonner Foundation. (n.d.). *History.* Retrieved from http://www.bonner.org/bonner-program-history/

Countryman, M., & Eatman, T. K. (2017). Connecting civil rights and community engagement: Intergenerational dimensions of resonating movements. In C. Dolgon, T. D. Mitchell, & T. K. Eatman (Eds.), *The Cambridge handbook of service learning and community engagement* (pp. 93–98). New York, NY: Cambridge University Press.

DEC: Downtown Education Collaborative. (n.d.). Retrieved from http://www.davidscobey.net/new-page-22

Deegan, M. J. (2017). Jane Addams, feminist pragmatism, and service learning. In C. Dolgon, T. D. Mitchell, & T. K. Eatman (Eds.), *The Cambridge handbook of service learning and community engagement* (pp. 51–63). New York, NY: Cambridge University Press.

Dees, J. G. (2001). *The meaning of "social entrepreneurship."* White paper. Retrieved from https://centers.fuqua.duke.edu/case/wp-content/uploads/sites/7/2015/03/Article_Dees_MeaningofSocialEntrepreneurship_2001.pdf

Ellison, J., & Eatman, T. K. (2008). *Scholarship in public: Knowledge creation and tenure policy in the engaged university.* Syracuse, NY: Imagining America.

Freire, P. (1970). *Pedagogy of the oppressed.* New York, NY: Continuum.

Goldberg, N. (2005). *Measuring the impact of microfinance: Taking stock of what we know.* Grameen Foundation USA.

Grameen Foundation. (n.d.). *About.* Retrieved from https://grameenfoundation.org/about

Hollander, E. L., Lapping, M., Rice, R. E., &Cruz, N. (2017). Talking about origins: Four stories of engagement. In C. Dolgon, T. D. Mitchell, & T. K. Eatman (Eds.), *The Cambridge handbook of service learning and community engagement* (pp. 20–41). New York, NY: Cambridge University Press.

Horton, M., Kohl, J., & Kohl, H. (1998). *The long haul: An autobiography.* New York, NY: Teachers College Press.

IMPACT National Conference. (n.d.). *History*. Retrieved from https://www.impactconference.org/about-the-conference/history/

Kahane, M. (2016, Summer). New challenge: Developing entrepreneurial leaders for social impact. *Diversity & Democracy, 19*(3).

Kelley, T., & Kelley, D. (2013). *Creative confidence: Unleashing the creative potential within us all*. New York, NY: Crown Business.

Kellogg Commission on the Future of State and Land-Grant Universities. (1999, February). *Returning to our roots: The engaged institution*. Washington, DC: National Association of State Universities and Land-Grant Colleges.

Kenny, M. E., & Gallagher, L. E. (2002). Service-learning: A history of systems. In M. E. Kenny, L. A. K. Simon, K. Kiley-Brabeck, & R. M. Lerner (Eds.), *Learning to serve: Promoting civil society through service learning* (pp. 15–29). New York, NY: Kluwer.

Kidder, T. (2003). *Mountains beyond mountains*. New York, NY: Random House.

Kim, M. (2015, August 4). *4 Evolutions in social innovation education happening now and the 4 evolutions to come*. Retrieved from http://ashokau.org/blog/4-evolutions-in-social-innovation-education-happening-now-and-the-4-evolutions-to-come/

Kim, M., & Krampetz, E. (2016, Summer). The rise of the sophisticated changemaker. *Diversity & Democracy, 19*(3).

Mills, C. W. (1956). *The power elite*. New York, NY: Oxford University Press.

Mills, C. W. (1959). *The sociological imagination*. New York, NY: Oxford University Press.

Milway, K. S., & Goulay, C. D. (2013, February 26). The rise of social entrepreneurship in B-schools in three charts. *Harvard Business Review*. Retrieved from https://hbr.org/2013/02/the-rise-of-social-entrepreneu

Moore, B. (1966). *Social origins of dictatorship and democracy: Lord and peasant in the making of the modern world*. Boston, MA: Beacon Press.

Museum L-A partnership. (n.d.). Retrieved from http://www.davidscobey.net/new-page-5

National Task Force on Civic Learning and Democratic Engagement. (2012). *A crucible moment: College learning and democracy's future*. Washington, DC: Association of American Colleges & Universities.

Roth, M. S. (2014). *Beyond the university: Why liberal education matters*. New Haven, CT: Yale University Press.

Saltmarsh, J., & Hartley, M. (2017). A brief history of the civic engagement movement in American higher education. In C. Dolgon, T. D. Mitchell, & T. K. Eatman (Eds.), *The Cambridge handbook of service learning and community engagement* (pp. 112–124). New York, NY: Cambridge University Press.

Saltmarsh, J., Hartley, M., & Clayton, P. (2009). *Democratic engagement white paper*. Boston, MA: New England Resource Center for Higher Education.

Sanchez, G. J. (2004). *Crossing Figueroa: The tangled web of diversity and democracy*. Syracuse, NY: Imagining America.

Schiller, B. (2015, March 10). Does microfinance actually work? *Fast Company*. Retrieved from https://www.fastcompany.com/3043301/does-microfinance-actually-work

Schon, D. A. (1983). *The reflective practitioner: How professionals think in action*. New York, NY: Basic Books.

Scobey, D. (2011). *Civic engagement and the Copernican moment*. Syracuse, NY: Imagining America.

Scobey, D. (2014a). *The gifts of liberal education*. Paper presented at Robertson Memorial Lecture, University of Michigan, Ann Arbor.

Scobey, D. (2014b). The invitation. *Public*, 2(1). Retrieved from http://public.imaginingamerica.org/blog/article/the-invitation/

Scobey, D. (2017). The frayed compact: American democracy, higher education, and the movement for community engagement. In C. Dolgon, T. D. Mitchell, & T. K. Eatman (Eds.), *The Cambridge handbook of service learning and community engagement* (pp. 511–526). New York, NY: Cambridge University Press.

Stanton, T. K., Giles, D. E., Jr., & Cruz, N. (Eds.). (1999). *Service-learning: A movement's pioneers reflect on its origins, practice, and future*. San Francisco, CA: Jossey-Bass.

Wallerstein, N., & Duran, B. (2008). The conceptual, historical, and practice roots of community-based participatory research and related participatory traditions. In M. Minkler & N. Wallerstein (Eds.), *Community-based participatory research for health: From process to outcomes* (pp. 27–52). San Francisco, CA: Jossey-Bass.

Wang, C. C., & Burris, M. A. (1997). Photovoice: Concept, methodology, and use for participatory needs assessment. *Health Education and Behavior, 24*(3), 369–387.

Wang, C. C., Cash, J. L., & Powers, L. S. (2000). Who knows the streets as well as the homeless? Promoting personal and community action through photovoice. *Health Promotion Practice* 1(1), 81–89.

Worsham, E. L. (2012). Reflections and insights on teaching social entrepreneurship: An interview with Greg Dees. *Academy of Management Learning and Education, 11*(3), 442–452.

Yunus, M. (1999). *Banker to the poor: The autobiography of Muhammad Yunus, founder of the Grameen Bank*. London, UK: Penguin Books.

Chapter Three

DIVERSITY AND DEMOCRATIC JUSTICE

Lost Compasses for Civic Engagement and Social Innovation

Caryn McTighe Musil

In 2005, I organized a preconference symposium called "Working Convergences: Liberal Education, Creativity, and the Entrepreneurial Spirit" before the annual meeting of the Association of American Colleges & Universities (AAC&U), where I was serving as senior vice president of the Office of Diversity, Equity, and Global Initiatives. Bill Drayton, who in 1980 founded Ashoka, a social entrepreneurship venture with the slogan "Everyone a changemaker," was the keynote speaker. In the spring of that same year, AAC&U's *Peer Review* was titled "Liberal Education and the Entrepreneurial Spirit" and included articles by Drayton and other symposium speakers. More than 13 years later, I consider convergences and divergences once again. The passage of time offers a clarifying moment for me.

In this volume, Eric Mlyn and Amanda Moore McBride are exploring the overlay and differences between civic engagement and social innovation. I remain uneasy now, as I was in 2005, that many of us, all too eager to emphasize the convergences and be good collaborative partners, are rushing toward unity without sufficient reflection. What might social innovation and civic engagement be paying too scant attention to in conception and practice? I will argue that both movements have, to their diminishment, ignored or underplayed the legacies and power of diversity as they also veered decidedly away from embracing democratic language, processes, structures, and aspirational values. The consequences are that students through social innovation are prepared to fix the world in their own, largely solo, vision, and students through civic engagement have inadequate preparation about diverse populations before working to address their unmet needs. Neither sufficiently prepares students to invest in fuller political collaborations across deep, historic differences and through democratic structures to establish collectively achieved democratic justice.

Ironically, for nearly five decades, through a variety of means, including the dramatic demographic shifts in who goes to college, campuses have offered students greater opportunities to study diversity and engage across differences. The emergence of more inclusive campus environments has, however, largely occurred apart from emergent movements for civic engagement and social innovation. To unyoke diversity from the other two has diluted civic engagement and social innovation's educational and political impact. It need not remain so.

Helping me pinpoint my discomfort at the 2005 symposium, my longtime national colleague Elizabeth Minnich whispered to me, "Neither Bill nor anyone else is using the word *democracy*." For my part, I felt uneasy because speakers had barely referred to diversity throughout the entire day. As context, both Minnich and I had been on the National Panel in the 1990s for the initial four-year project within an AAC&U initiative called "American Commitments: Diversity, Democracy, and Liberal Learning." In my responsibilities at AAC&U, from 1992 to 2002, I was a leader of this initiative which generated a series of grants that ultimately involved hundreds of colleges and universities, especially in curriculum redesign, faculty development, and institutional change. A series of monographs, which the National Panel had composed by 1995, offered new intellectual frameworks for higher education as it was moving away from its long history of apartheid education toward more multicultural, multiracial, and inclusive colleges and universities. This included what knowledge is taught and by whom, who the students are, and in what kind of institutional environment deeper learning occurs. The National Panel challenged the commonly accepted binary that a college could have *either* excellence *or* diversity. We argued that excellence could be achieved only *through* diversity.

AAC&U published the following three monographs in 1995: *The Drama of Diversity and Democracy: Higher Education and American Commitments* (AAC&U, 1995b); *Liberal Learning and the Arts of Connection for the New Academy* (AAC&U, 1995c); and *American Pluralism and the*

College Curriculum (AAC&U, 1995a). AAC&U's distinctive contribution to others' earlier national investigations of diversity was to couple diversity with democracy. Values of equality, dignity, liberty, justice, and equal opportunity are at the core of U.S. democracy in the abstract. They have yet to be in practice for all Americans. Diversity has called repeatedly on democracy to account for patterned inequities. Denied the right to participate equally in U.S. democracy, different groups have used stated democratic values to claim full citizenship, whether White women seeking equal suffrage; African Americans working to end slavery, undo Jim Crow, or pass legislation aimed to protect their civil rights; or Japanese Americans demanding reparations for being forcibly moved to mass incarceration centers and unfairly stripped of their rights and property as citizens.

As attracted as I was to the 2005 symposium's provocative solutions-oriented framing, my discomfort with social entrepreneurship was triggered by its apparent erasure of diversity and any recognition of how the accompanying stratifications of race, class, gender, or other differences devaluing certain groups affected access to opportunity, voice, recognition, and influence. In Drayton's articulation, all individuals were equally capable of being changemakers facing similar challenges, similar access to power, and similar likelihood of being heard. The ethical centerpiece of Drayton's inspiring talk was a dramatic visual of global economic inequality, in which "50 percent of the world's people have 5 percent of the world's income. This is not fair, sustainable, or safe. But this is reality. And this reality is really where the Ashoka idea begins" (Drayton, 2005, p. 8). He then proposed, "Everybody should see him or herself as a changemaker. Once so empowered, a person can do anything" (p. 9). Defying overwhelming evidence to the contrary, the argument presumed everyone began on the same starting block and would wield the same influence. Other than noting economic inequality as a global challenge, diversity was then abandoned as a factor to consider for the rest of the speech.

In the symposium, I was equally troubled by the social entrepreneurship advocates' reliance on the individual actor void of a political context, yet whose charge was to conceive of a great idea and then convince enough other people to implement it in order to change systems. The solutions were, it seemed, resting like seed corn in the fertile brain/character/imagination of a single social entrepreneur in a disquieting, undemocratic hierarchy that echoed the Elizabethan Great Chain of Being. That is, the individual social entrepreneur alone had both the vision and the fix. They were not obligated as one might be in a democratically constructed process to create a compelling idea in conversation with, let alone surrender to, others who might have better ideas. Moreover, so driven by a charismatic individual, the process was devoid of reliance on democratic practices through which one might ensure that everyone was attended to as problems were identified, remedies proposed, and solutions implemented.

I experienced a similar disquiet in a 2003 Wingspread conference on civic engagement and research universities sponsored by the University of Michigan. A group of leaders from the contemporary civic engagement movement, almost all of whom were White and male, met with a group largely from AAC&U's American Commitments National Panel, who represented women and men across race, ethnicity, class backgrounds, and sexual identities. The gathering sought to explore where there might be correspondences with what was emerging as a strong movement that labeled itself as civic engagement and an equally strong movement for diversity, the latter driven in its actions by democratic aspirational principles, practices, and pedagogies. On college campuses, each of the two movements had set up centers, spawned new curricula, hired new faculty and staff, employed newly appointed administrators, and engaged with communities and social issues both within and beyond the boundaries of the campus. Yet their efforts were parallel, not integrative, and with a few rare exceptions their programs had little interaction.

Tensions grew during the Wingspread meeting, culminating when the civic engagement leaders asserted that in an age of disaffection people needed to reclaim their democratic citizenship that had eroded over time. Diversity leaders were affronted by such nostalgia for a past when only a sliver of White men had been granted rights to democratic citizenship, by an utter failure to notice the privileged positions shaping the meeting leaders' language, and by how easily the meeting leaders had glossed over the violence that kept such democratic disenfranchisement in place. In other conversations, tensions surfaced when civic engagement leaders assured diversity leaders that it was not necessary to begin by recognizing differences because working together on a shared goal would take care of differentials and disparities. Diversity leaders argued that understanding differentials of experience, history, culture, and recognition was a necessary initial framework. Unacknowledged, it would affect the group process as well as the outcome. If social innovators rushed too quickly in solo efforts to devise the solution for a communal problem, civic engagement practitioners rushed too quickly to move collectively to devise civic solutions assuming differences did not matter.

Shortly after the new millenium began, then, both social entrepreneurship and civic engagement limited their effectiveness and certainly their inclusiveness by either downplaying democracy and its aspirational goals and processes or largely ignoring diversity and its history—or sometimes both. Each needed to pay more attention to the twin compasses of diversity and democratic justice as they designed programs, procedures, conceptual frameworks, and scholarship and sought to transform their institutions and the larger world. Without including diversity and democratic justice, alliances with community, business, and government agencies would be undermined, as would a collective ability to address wicked challenges globally and locally.

Diversity and Democratic Justice as Navigation Instruments

We discovered in "American Commitments" that coupling diversity and democracy generates tensions that create "an obscured, too often forgotten, context for engaging pervasive issues of difference and inclusion in our country" (AAC&U, 1995b, p. 9). *The Drama of Diversity and Democracy* (AAC&U, 1995b) argued, "When diversity is characterized by patterned inequities and persistent marginalization, it is a symptom of democracy's failure, a sign of society's unwillingness or inability to confront continuing injustices" (p. 10). For its part, democratic values provide "a moral compass—by which a society can be held accountable" (p. 10). The National Panel insisted on the inextricable relationship of the two: "As we ignite anew the republic's democratic creed and ideals it shapes of a just society . . . we must move toward an understanding of community intersections, of profound interdependence, and of our continuing need for one another's experiences and contributions" (p. 33). If both scholars and practitioners of social innovation and civic engagement used this navigator's tool as they mapped their respective fields, it could have transformative effects on the processes adopted; goals articulated; and impact on learners, communities, and social compacts, both locally and globally.

In *American Pluralism and the College Curriculum* (AAC&U, 1995a), diversity and democracy are interwoven in a set of three thematic recommendations. It offers blueprints that could serve as grounded knowledge for contemporary civic engagement and social innovation programs. The National Panel's first recommendation was that every college student have an opportunity through a variety of courses to explore "EXPERIENCE, IDENTITY, AND ASPIRATION: The study of one's own particular inherited and constructed traditions, identity communities, and significant questions, in their complexity" (p. 25). How to do that could vary from writing courses to literature, history, sociology, art, or performance. Such widespread interrogations invite students to learn from one another about the collective composite of "We the People." The second general recommendation for necessary knowledge gained through a multitude of inventive curricular options was "UNITED STATES PLURALISM AND THE PURSUITS OF JUSTICE: An extended and comparative exploration of diverse peoples in this society, with significant attention to their differing experiences of United States democracy and the pursuits . . . of equal opportunity" (p. 25). Consider how divergent this language is from words typically adopted by either civic engagement or social innovation programs. The third recommendation could be achieved through experiential courses. These differentiated themselves from most service-learning frameworks at that time and were described as "EXPERIENCES IN JUSTICE SEEKING: Encounters with systemic constraints on the development of human potential in the United States and experiences in community-based efforts to articulate principles of justice, expand opportunity, and redress inequities" (p. 25).

In this experiential model, the report insists it is essential that colleges "work collaboratively *from the start* with local groups (official or disenfranchised) in defining a mutually attractive agenda" (AAC&U, 1995a, p. 37, emphasis in original) as students learn more about communities where the promise of democracy has been largely denied. The stance of the student is not, then, as the grand changemaker to whom others should defer but rather an inquisitive, humble learner, listening respectfully to what others describe as their lived experiences, everyday challenges, and deepest unfilled aspirations. From that immersive experience in perspective taking, the student would then work alongside these stakeholders on a specific issue. The experiences in justice seeking model diverged from early service-learning practices of outreach suggesting the college had the best ideas for addressing social inequities. Instead, AAC&U's (1995a) justice-seeking recommendation came closer to where the civic engagement movement has evolved to 25 years later in its embrace of affirming the value of generative, reciprocal, mutually respectful partnerships so that college and community representatives can collaborate more equitably to address society's pressing problems. Social innovation shows some movement but has a longer trek to make.

While AAC&U sought to keep diversity and democratic justice inseparable in the 1990s, the civic engagement movement unraveled the knot that bound the two. Social innovation seemed to have never bound them. The choice of language for these new movements accelerated the erosion of bonds: the language of *service* and *civic* for civic engagement; the language of *innovation* and *solutions* for social innovation. Certainly, these softer and trendier terms have contributed to the respective meteoric rises of the two movements on college campuses, but there has been a price. Diversity was edged almost entirely off stage. Community became the lexicon describing the arena of either civic action or invention, largely abandoning the lens of a diverse democracy and democratic justice in their wake.

For their part, the social innovation websites are largely democracy- and justice-free territories. Instead the language of business dominates as programs accentuate performance, entrepreneurship, incubators, capitalization strategies, impact, disruption, and bold actions. In most descriptions, people do not exist, but problems do—and they are pressing. In fact, the only people described are the students, void of any distinctive cultural markers, but seen, as the late and influential Duke professor J. Gregory Dees (2001) explains, as social innovators with "a vision of how to achieve improvement and they are determined to make their vision work." Social innovators are described as leaders who represent the brightest minds. They are consultants with expertise, not citizens with mutual responsibilities to work collectively for the public good. There is no indication that the innovators should be accountable to the *people* enmeshed in the problems that the innovators are so committed to solving. The erasure of people, of course, makes it easier to omit diversity as a category of analysis.

A Crucible Moment: Rediscovering the Warp and Woof of Diversity and Democracy

In 2010, The Global Perspective Institute Inc., a small research business run by Larry A. Braskamp, emeritus professor at Loyola University of Chicago and senior fellow at AAC&U, collaborated on a proposal with the Office of Diversity, Equity, and Global Initiatives at AAC&U, which I headed at the time. The Department of Education through Under Secretary Martha Kanter awarded us a grant to explore the state of civic learning and democratic engagement on college campuses. We were charged with examining how well higher education was preparing new generations of informed, responsible citizens and with determining how we could accelerate progress and reach more students. It ultimately became a watershed moment and resulted in a landmark report, *A Crucible Moment: College Learning and Democracy's Future* (National Task Force on Civic Learning and Democratic Engagement, 2012).

A series of national roundtable meetings gathered diverse stakeholders from civic organizations off campus, civic centers and practitioners on campuses, social innovation organizations, diversity leaders, students, presidents, scholars, researchers, disciplinary societies, government agencies, and foundations. They assessed academia's commitment to education for a diverse democracy; where and to what degree democratic engagement had become integrated into a student's college experience; who outside higher education could exert influence; and what recommendations might make such opportunities expected for all students, everywhere, across levels and departments. Most important, the pause for a thorough self-examination also opened the opportunity to reattach diversity and democratic justice as recommended normative practices in the civic engagement movement.

The national roundtables also brought attention to a previous national report that ultimately anchored *A Crucible Moment. Higher Education for American Democracy*, produced by the President's Commission on Higher Education (1947) appointed by President Truman, was the treasure trove that also linked diversity and democratic justice. In the aftermath of witnessing the collapse of almost every European democracy by the onslaught of fascism in World War II, the economic devastation in Europe and Asia, and the unsettling capacity of human beings on all sides to annihilate and degrade one another on an unprecedented scale, the United States took bold steps to build democratic governments and institutions, ensure economic recovery, and cultivate more compassionate and equitable human understandings of one another. While the Marshall Plan sowed the seeds of economic rebirth in Europe, the President's Commission on Higher Education sowed the seeds of democracy's promise through higher education. Recalibrating higher education's compass, the commission declared, "The first and most essential charge upon higher education is that at all levels and in all its fields of specialization, it shall be the carrier of democratic values, ideals, and process" (President's Commission on Higher Education, 1947, p. 102). The commission singled out the following principal goals "which should come first in our time":

- Education for a fuller realization of democracy in every phase of living.
- Education directly and explicitly for international understanding and cooperation.
- Education for the application of creative imagination and trained intelligence to the solution of social problems and to the administration of public affairs (p. 19).

The realization of democracy, the importance of global responsibility, and the application of knowledge to address the world's pressing problems represent a triad that should guide today's civic engagement and social innovation movements.

If the language, principles, values, and processes of *democracy*—not civic engagement or social innovation—were given the highest priority in the commission's recommendations, diversity and democratic justice were deemed to be inextricably linked. Racial subjugation and discrimination in economic and social life in America at midcentury were utterly normalized and tolerated. So, too, was an apartheid higher education system in every U.S. geographic location, though enforced by law and violence in the South. Most of the commission's members came to recognize that these realities prevented the United States from legitimately claiming its role as leader of freedom and democracy. Acknowledging this, the commission labeled racial discrimination as "an undemocratic practice" (President's Commission on Higher Education, 1947, p. 25) and took a defiant stand, asserting the following:

> No more in mind than body can this nation or any endure half slave, half free. Education that liberates and ennobles must be equally available to all. Justice to the individual demands this; the safety and progress of the nation depend upon it. (p. 101)

It would take more than two decades to make progress undoing deeply entrenched racial segregation, and another two more to achieve significant racial and cultural diversity in college and university students, but this 1947 commission report unmistakably drew a line in the sand.

A Crucible Moment argues that the President's Commission was the first in a long line of democratic influences on higher education between 1947 and 2010 that braided diversity and democratic justice. It is a history that clashes with early and even contemporary accounts from many of the most respected leaders and scholars of the civic engagement movement, including some in this volume, who stubbornly continue to mark the origins of the civic engagement movement in 1985 when Campus Compact was founded. Doing so dangerously distorts the real origins and actors of democratic engagement in higher education. The 1960s and 1970s witnessed transformative political movements in the United States that led to sweeping national legislation correcting in part centuries of inequality, especially regarding race and gender. On campuses, more richly diverse student populations began to have access to higher education in the four decades after World War II and drove the rise in more active political and social engagement in public issues. Erasing this history has contributed to isolating civic engagement from diversity as an educational movement, as the following paragraph explains.

Soon after the war, the GI Bill made higher education no longer the exclusive privilege of middle- and upper-class people. The bill subsidized veterans who represented primarily working-class people, multiple ethnicities and faiths, and the initial though smaller group of African Americans. The diversification of students was further enhanced by the power of the civil rights movement in the 1950s and 1960s; the passage of the Civil Rights Act of 1964 and the Immigration and Nationality Act of 1965; the emergence of the Black Power movement in the 1960s and 1970s; Title IX; and the arrival of the second, third, and fourth waves of the women's movement in the 1960s through today, corresponding to a demographic shift that made women the majority of college students by the late 1970s.

Creating the national network of public community college systems in the 1970s and 1980s, another recommendation from the Truman Commission, has further transformed the demographic profile of higher education. Disability legislation passed in the 1970s that accelerated access and accommodation on campuses; more students openly identifying as gay, lesbian, bisexual, transgendered, or queer, thus challenging heterosexual norms; dramatic growth of the population of international students; and the surfacing of unparalleled religious diversity, challenging the singular centrality of Christian campus chapels have all combined to make student diversity a norm today on almost every American college campus. These students were largely brought into that educational marketplace of ideas because social movements seeking democratic justice had preceded their entrance. This is the much longer, diversity-driven democratic history that should be informing the historical narratives of civic engagement and social innovation programs. However, unfortunately, the largely White male civic engagement origin narrative continues to be told and retold, writing out of history the very democratic movements that made it possible for civic engagement to gain a footing.

A Crucible Moment reminds us that when the rich diversity of people and perspectives are acknowledged as the nutrients that alter knowledge and action, higher education can then be transformed into

> an intellectual and public commons where it is possible not only to theorize about what education for democratic citizenship might require in a diverse society, but also to rehearse that citizenship daily in the fertile, roiling context of pedagogic inquiry and hands-on experience. (National Task Force, p. 2)

To do that well whether on campus or off in the twenty-first century clearly required a reboot on what had previously been understood as a sufficient way to define *education for citizenship*. Therefore, one of the five essential actions *A Crucible Moment* recommended was to "advance a contemporary, comprehensive framework for civic learning—embracing U.S. and global interdependence—that includes historic and modern understandings of democratic values, capacities to engage diverse perspectives and people, and commitment to collective civic problem solving" (p. vi). The larger framing was expanded in part through and because of diversity that was beginning to be understood as a vehicle for achieving democratic culture and democratic justice.

The framework that emerged from the national roundtables and campus practices even if not yet sufficiently put in place pays homage to diversity and democracy's coupling. When talking about what kind of knowledge would be required to educate students for twenty-first-century civic learning and democratic engagement, the list was rich in pluralism and freshly recast democratic investigations. Students, the report posited, needed to acquire the following:

- Familiarity with key democratic texts and universal democratic principles, and with selected debates—in US and other societies—concerning their applications;
- Historical and sociological understanding of several democratic movements, both US and abroad;
- Understanding one's sources of identity and their influence on civic values, assumptions, and responsibilities to a wider public;
- Knowledge of the diverse cultures, histories, values, and contestations that have shaped US and other world societies;
- Exposure to multiple religious traditions and to alternative views about the relation between religion and government;
- Knowledge of the political systems that frame constitutional democracies and of political levers for influencing change. (National Task Force, p. 4)

This indeed firmly establishes a commitment to diversity and democratic justice as necessary to today's civic engagement movement in higher education. The navigational charts are mapped out. Now the practice must catch up with the charts.

Research on Diversity and Democracy: A Compelling Coupling

If *A Crucible Moment* helped to rebraid diversity and democracy within the civic engagement movement, a critical cadre of diversity researchers provided evidence of how diversity is deeply tied to democratic outcomes. Among the most prolific and influential, Sylvia Hurtado began in the mid-1990s to couple research on diversity with student learning and ultimately with outcomes essential to a diverse democracy and workforce. Hurtado's (2003) pioneering publication, "Preparing College Students for a Diverse Democracy," involved 10 large public research universities. When she released her formal report in 2003, Hurtado had already secured the endorsement of AAC&U, Campus Compact, and what was then called the Office of Minorities in Higher Education at American Council on Education. The illuminating research that investigates how diversity leads to democratic outcomes, therefore, has been available to civic and social innovation practitioners for more than a decade. "This project," she writes in her final report, "addresses how campuses are creating diverse learning environments to prepare students to become full participants in a diverse democracy" (p. iii). She goes on to assert how the report "replicates previous findings and extends the research that links diversity with the teaching/learning and public service mission of higher education" (p. v) and shows "the tremendous benefits that can be achieved in creating diverse learning environments that prepare students for citizenship in a complex, and increasingly diverse society" (p. v).

Cognitive and social development theory had long asserted that active and critical thinking accelerated when a person's embedded beliefs, worldviews, and behaviors were interrupted by knowledge that called everything into question. Hurtado and others immediately recognized how the diversity of people, perspectives, and subjects/authors of study in college also possessed that catalytic effect. Research accumulated revealing how experiences of diversity produced necessary skills for a diverse democracy, such as perspective taking, a belief that conflict enhances democratic culture-building, and a commitment to engage in collective social action. Other researchers came to similar conclusions.

Larry Braskamp and Mark Engberg (2011) determined that students who had diversity courses demonstrated an "acceptance of multiple perspectives in their thinking and knowing" and "demonstrated a strong preference toward cross-cultural interaction and making a difference in society" (p. 3). Hurtado, Ruiz, and Whang (2012) found similar results about the correlation between an inclusive curriculum and students developing a "pluralist orientation . . . , perspective taking, tolerance of different beliefs, openness to having their views challenged, ability to negotiate controversial issues, and ability to work cooperatively with diverse people" (p. 11). Moreover, the Diverse Learning Environments Survey developed by the Higher Education Research Institute (2019) at UCLA, where Hurtado had served as director, continues to generate research illuminating the connection between diversity and democratic outcomes.

Similarly, in a major research project spearheaded by Gurin, Nagda, and Sorensen (2011) involving 52 different academically based intergroup dialogue courses in which two major diverse subjects—such as gender and race or race and religion—were matched by a diverse group of student participants, the short- and long-term effects on students were confirmed. These intergroup dialogue courses had profound and lasting impacts on democratic dispositions, skills, and political commitments. Some of the research findings included the following outcomes: greater increases in understanding race, gender, and income inequality; intergroup empathy and motivation to bridge differences; greater increases in the efficacy and frequency of their intergroup action during college; and commitment to postcollege social and political action.

Capitalizing on Synergies: Collective Problem-Solving, Partnerships, and a Student's Major

A hopeful sign today is the increasing evidence, especially within civic engagement programs, that many campuses have begun to reframe their aims and processes toward more democratic partnerships with others. They have also begun to acknowledge programmatically the power of deploying diverse people, perspectives, and stakeholders to more effectively tackle big, thorny issues. Integrating diversity and democratic justice intentionally, transparently, and by design into civic engagement and social innovation programs could in the coming decade have a transformative impact on how prepared students will be to become the democratic changemakers both movements so aspire to. Nevertheless, each needs to make diversity an essential, not optional, part of their program of study, integrating some of the curricular frameworks that the American Commitments panel and *American Pluralism and the College Curriculum* monograph described earlier. If economics and technology are expected parts of the social innovation programs, so should academic inquiries about diversity and democracy. Similarly, if reflection is so integral to service-learning, surely the study of the racial, cultural, and social history of the communities where students and faculty may be engaged should take equal priority. In addition, incorporating some of the twenty-first-century frameworks offered by *A Crucible Moment* that entwine diversity and democracy offers additional curricular pathways and pedagogies that should be understood as necessary for both civic engagement and social innovation.

Two examples that show how such a vision is emerging are represented by California State University, Monterey Bay (CSUMB) for civic engagement and by Ashoka U for social innovation. The latter refers to the network of 45 colleges and universities from around the globe designated as Changemaker Campuses by Ashoka U, a program launched in 2008 as an initiative within its parent organization, Ashoka. CSUMB was the only service-learning program AAC&U could find in the late 1990s that had identified diversity as 1 of the 3 essential conceptual framings for its community-based work. Its director, Seth Pollack, has continued to be a national and global leader in the field. In what is an even more nuanced framework today, Pollack's Service Learning Prism (CSUMB, n.d.) guides the development of service-learning courses required at 2 levels for every student at CSUMB: first as an introductory course within general education for every student and then in an upper level course connected to a student's major. The prism involves the following sides: justice, diversity, and social responsibility. Compassion is identified as grounding all 3. Discipline-based knowledge, student knowledge, and community knowledge traverse the prism to be transformed into new knowledge, skills, and awareness of self and society.

Ashoka U has created a manifesto that guides the values in its 45 campuses designated as Changemaker Campuses. The manifesto moves beyond promoting only the single brilliant fixer of all problems. Instead, it articulates as values a commitment to "empowering students to lead and develop the skills of empathy, distributed leadership, collaboration and creative problem solving" and "building mutually beneficial partnerships with local and global communities" in order to "contribute to the vitality of people and the planet" (Ashoka U, n.d.). The language of democracy is still missing, but more of its collaborative, partnering, collective values are named. Diversity, alas, remains largely absent as a category.

There are three arenas for future expansion where diversity and democratic justice could become central to civic engagement and social innovation as they begin to chart their future decades of work. All three were recommended in *A Crucible Moment* where social innovation was lightly present at roundtable discussions through involvement by Ashoka, Mobilize.org, Innovations in Civic Participation, and The Guiding Lights Network, even if the dominant representation overall was from the explosive field of civic engagement. The three shared arenas for productive strategic focus are the following:

1. Problem-solving and collective action
2. Development of robust, generative off-campus partnerships to address common problems and empower people to act

3. The largely unclaimed space of a student's major for creating more comprehensive, integrative experiences to enact democratic enterprises with others to achieve a more just world

Problem-Solving and Collective Action

In its more comprehensive twenty-first-century framework for civic learning in *A Crucible Moment*, collective action moved civic learning from the traditionally more passive, sideline stance of studying *about* democracy, as a noun, to enacting it, as a verb.

> [F]ull civic literacies cannot be garnered only by studying books. . . . Democratic knowledge and capabilities also are honed through hands-on, face-to-face active engagement in the midst of differing perspectives about how to address common problems that affect the well-being of the nation and the world. (National Task Force, 2012, p. 3)

In the national report, a chart called "What Would a Civic-Minded Campus Look Like?" includes the following explanation of *civic action* as lifelong practice:

> The capacity and commitment both to participate constructively with diverse others and to work collectively to address common problems; the practice of working in a pluralistic society and world to improve the quality of people's lives and the sustainability of the planet; the ability to analyze systems in order to plan and engage in public action; the moral and political courage to take risks to achieve a greater public good. (National Task Force, 2012, p. 15)

Achieving these democratic collaborative skills cannot be accomplished without a diversity lens as part of public problem-solving, which could, in turn, lead to more humane, just, and flourishing societies. Therefore, both civic engagement and social innovation programs need to design knowledge and experience of diversity and democratic justice into their respective curriculum and pedagogies, as both are driven by addressing pressing societal dilemmas.

Promoting such a shift in solving such problems, John Saltmarsh and Matthew Hartley (2011) called for transitioning from a civic engagement to a democratic engagement paradigm, which they felt would transfer the focus from activity and place to purpose and process. They describe the transformative power of being driven by democratic values:

> Democratic engagement locates the university within an ecosystem of knowledge production, requiring interaction with other knowledge producers outside the university for the creation of new problem-solving knowledge through a multidirectional flow of knowledge expertise. In this paradigm, students learn cooperative and creative problem solving within learning environments in which faculty, students, and individuals from the community work and deliberate together. . . . Civic engagement in the democratic-centered paradigm is intentionally political in that students learn about democracy by acting democratically. (p. 21)

Generative Partnerships

There has been a dynamic evolution of campus/community partnerships driven by civic engagement and, to some extent, social innovation programs. *A Crucible Moment* pinpointed building strong partnerships as one of the five essential actions that needed to be taken if civic learning and democratic engagement were to be transformative for not only students but also the community and the way academia understands and fulfills its mission. The recommendation in *A Crucible Moment* reads, "Expand the number of robust, generative civic partnerships and alliances, locally, nationally, and globally to address common problems, empower people to act, strengthen communities and nations, and generate new frontiers of knowledge" (National Task Force, 2012, p. vi). The national report argued that such a commitment must be shared across multiple sectors and actors and is required if the country is to "provide all students with the kind of education that will prepare them to take active responsibility both for the quality of our communities and for the future—U.S. and global—of . . . democracy" (p. 30).

It has become commonplace to see terms such as *reciprocal relationships, mutual benefits, cocreation,* and *impact on communities* used when discussing partnerships. While the language has certainly shifted, the learning on both sides continues to reflect how difficult it is to practice such behavior routinely. Models of how to develop robust, reciprocal partnerships have emerged in the scholarship, represented by scholars such as Andy Furco and Emily Jahnke as they describe the altered nature of partnerships moving from more transactional one-way streets to thicker, generative relationships that move from reaching out *to* the community, or working *on* community issues, to engaging *with* the community. In the last decade, Tania D. Mitchell has produced scholarship offering much needed frameworks for looking critically at the equity, power, and racial and class dynamics of partnerships. As Nancy Cantor and Peter Englot

(2015) describe this new diversity-rich, democratically driven problem-solving, they offer more insights:

> The commitment not only to space and professional staff but to continuously engaging a broadly inclusive "community of experts" is absolutely essential to the on-the-ground success of these projects, programs, and generative partnerships . . . [that build] on decades of work in intergroup dialogue and mounting evidence about the value of diversity in public problem solving . . . [especially] when we deliberately work to put those differences on the table in structured conversations. (pp. 77–79)

There are emerging models that embody many of the characteristics of what democratically driven, justice-seeking, reciprocal partnerships might look like. They involve big out-of-the-box thinking that social innovators are drawn to and trained in, but they are bound from inception to implementation by deep communal commitments to promote the common good. The Anchor Institutions Task Force (AITF), led by the University of Pennsylvania since 2009 and managed by Margo Incorporated, offers one model. The AITF accrues layered, place-based larger entities, such as universities and colleges, hospitals, key employers, community leaders, and often city government agencies that band together to invest political, cultural, economic, and intellectual capital to build stronger communities. Another formulation is found in Community-Campus Partnerships for Health (CCPH), a nonprofit entity founded in 1997 that represents a webbed network of health care delivery systems, colleges and universities, community-based organizations, foundations, and government partners. CCPH (n.d.) asserts that they believe "in the transformative power of partnerships. Our key initiatives are innovative and collaborative programs that advance healthy equity and social justice." CCPH clearly demonstrates how to integrate fully the language and practice of innovation and the partnership of civic engagement while also affirming democratic and diversity values of equity and social justice.

A recent example of civic engagement and social innovation guided by the twin compasses of diversity and democratic justice can be seen in the reimagined and repurposed 1901 Hahne & Co Building, an art deco landmark department store on the National Register of Historic Places that had been vacant since 1987 in downtown Newark, New Jersey. Shared space for everyone emerged as a result of public, private, and nonprofit groups, including Rutgers University–Newark (RU-N); $178 million in renovation; and deep conversations beforehand and ongoing with community leaders about how to do economic development that does not displace historic neighborhoods but empowers them. RU-N committed with community partners to creating Express Newark, a hub for arts and technical innovation with video, print, photography, and art galleries; classroom space; and its Department of Arts, Culture, and Media. The results affirm the power of coupling diversity and democratic opportunity with civic engagement and social innovation:

> Redeveloping the abandoned space as a distinctive, community-based educational program, [Rutgers University-Newark in partnership with] KSS designed an art incubator, community media center, portrait studio, design consortium, and letterpress studio. Community partnerships are numerous, including charter schools, county and city colleges, boys and girls clubs, the city museum, and local professional artists. With new activities every week, the center is a beacon of diversity and long-lasting economic and cultural viability, drawing together people of all ages, ethnicities, and occupations—utilizing the Arts as a common bond. For [RU-N], as an anchor institution in Newark, it is through the thoughtfully crafted relationship between architecture and community that the fabric of its urban neighborhood will strengthen and empower its citizenry. (Hahne & Co. Express Newark, 2017)

These kinds of newly created spaces are neither exclusively academic nor community but hybrid space cocreated into a more generative public square. In this participatory, inclusive location, "multiplicity of voices and perspectives becomes the norm; defining common purposes, needs, and processes is understood as a shared and contested goal"; and the partners address "large, systemic, public problems . . . through inventive, constructive, and mutually agreed upon solutions" (National Task Force, 2012, pp. 64–65).

Culminating Capstone Work in a Student's Major

With the expansion of civic problem-solving, action-oriented challenges to enact democratic justice and the investment in sustained reciprocal, generative partnerships, might the untilled land of the major also turn into fertile ground for democratic citizenship and the promotion through collective action of a more flourishing and equitable society and world?

A principal recommendation from *A Crucible Moment* argues that a student's major is ideal academic territory for anchoring civic learning and democratic engagement into purposeful pathways from first year to fourth year and in ways that challenge students to apply their learning to real-world situations (National Task Force, 2012). The national report elaborated, "Define within departments, programs, and disciplines the public purposes of their respective fields, the civic inquiries most urgent to explore, and the best way to infuse civic learning outcomes progressively across the major" (p. 32).

Conclusion

Both social innovation programs and their older cousins, civic engagement programs, have spent too much of their brief academic lives shy about acknowledging their kinship, let alone collaborating in cooking dinner together for the larger family. Hindering their impact and their transformative potential, they have each also spent too much time uncoupled from diversity and democratic justice as their moral compass for processes and purpose. That need not continue. Research on the power of diversity to accelerate education for engaged, responsible, committed democratic citizenship makes too compelling a case to ignore. Ripe opportunities through civic problem-solving and collective action, generative reciprocal democratic partnerships, and capstone culminating projects in a student's major—all offer untold chances for invention, creativity, and justice reaping in newly imagined and emerging collaborations.

Under the visionary leadership of President Nancy Cantor, RU-N produced its 2014 strategic plan. It did so using what Cantor refers to as an "'outside-in' view of what our state, nation, and world need from us" (Rutgers University–Newark, 2014, p. 4) and gathered insights from listening tours on and off campus, town halls, and structured dialogues. The language of the strategic plan resonates with phrases evoking diversity, democratic justice, invention, risk taking, big ideas, and commitment to civic space and the common good. It is all there. One delicious soup. The plan sets out what is possible to aspire to:

> We rely upon our colleges and universities to be engines of innovation and social mobility as well as educators of our democratic citizenry. We call upon them to think expansively and deeply about the pressing and increasingly interconnected challenges faced in every city, state, and nation; to prepare increasingly diverse generations of students for their roles in the workplaces . . . and in . . . public squares . . . ; to partner beyond their gates to magnify societal impact and create two-way streets of access and opportunity. (p. 5)

What in the world are we waiting for?

References

Anchor Institutions Task Force. (n.d.) https://margainc.com/aitf

Ashoka U. (n.d.). *Manifesto.* Retrieved from http://ashokau.org/changemaker-campus/manifesto/

Association of American Colleges & Universities. (1995a). *American pluralism and the college curriculum.* Washington, DC: Author.

Association of American Colleges & Universities. (1995b). *The drama of diversity and democracy: Higher education and American commitments.* Washington, DC: Author.

Association of American Colleges & Universities. (1995c). *Liberal learning and the arts of connection for the new academy.* Washington, DC: Author.

Association of American Colleges & Universities. (2017, Fall). *Peer Review, 19*(4). Retrieved from https://www.aacu.org/peerreview/2017/Fall

Association of American Colleges & Universities. (2018). *Case studies: Civic learning in the major by design.* Retrieved from https://www.aacu.org/case-studies-civic-learning-major-design

Braskamp, L. A., & Engberg, M. E. (2011). How colleges can influence the development of a global perspective. *Liberal Education, 97*(3/4), 34–39.

California State University, Monterey Bay. (n.d.). *The SL prism.* Retrieved from https://csumb.edu/service/sl-prism

Cantor, N., & Englot, P. (2015). Reinventing scholar educators as citizens and public workers. In H. C. Boyte (Ed.), *Democracy's education: Public work, citizenship, and the future of colleges and universities* (pp. 75–79). Nashville, TN: Vanderbilt University Press.

Community-Campus Partnerships for Health. (n.d.) https://www.ccphealth.org/ccph-key-initiatives/

Dees, J. G. (2001, May 30). *The meaning of "social entrepreneurship."* Retrieved from https://entrepreneurship.duke.edu/news-item/the-meaning-of-social-entrepreneurship/

Drayton, B. (2005). Everyone a changemaker. *Peer Review, 7*(3), 8–11.

Gurin, P., Nagda, B. A., & Sorensen, N. (2011). Intergroup dialogue: Education for a broad conception of civic engagement. *Liberal Education, 97*(2), 46–51.

Hahne & Co. Express Newark. (2017, April 21). *ARCHITECT, the Journal of the American Institute of Architects.* Retrieved from http://www.architectmagazine.com/project-gallery/hahne-co-express-newark

Higher Education Research Institute. (2019). Diverse Learning Environments Survey. Retrieved from https://heri.ucla.edu/diverse-learning-environments-survey/

Hurtado, S. (2003). *Preparing college students for a diverse democracy.* Final report to the U.S. Department of Education, OERI, Field Initiated Studies Program. Ann Arbor, MI: Center for the Study of Higher and Postsecondary Education. Retrieved from http://citeseerx.ist.psu.edu/viewdoc/download?doi=10.1.1.511.1225&rep=rep1&type=pdf

Hurtado, S., Ruiz, A., & Whang, H. (2012). Advancing and assessing civic learning: New results for the diversity learning environments survey. *Diversity & Democracy*, 15(3), 10–12.

National Task Force on Civic Learning and Democratic Engagement. (2012). *A crucible moment: College learning and democracy's future*. Washington, DC: Association of American Colleges & Universities.

President's Commission on Higher Education. (1947). *Higher education for American democracy, Vol. I, Establishing the goals*. Washington, DC: Government Printing Office.

Rutgers University–Newark. (2014). *Where opportunity meets excellence: Strategic plan 2014*. Retrieved from http://www.newark.rutgers.edu/sites/default/files/run_strategic_plan_-final.pdf

Saltmarsh, J., & Hartley, M. (Eds.). (2011). *"To serve a larger purpose": Engagement for democracy and the transformation of higher education*. Philadelphia, PA: Temple University Press.

Chapter Four

EXPLORATORY STUDY ON STUDENTS' PERCEPTIONS ABOUT SERVICE-LEARNING AND SOCIAL ENTREPRENEURSHIP

Joan Clifford, David Malone, Amy Anderson, Dane Emmerling, and Evan Widney

There exists within the current landscape of higher education a widespread belief in "higher education's civic mission and its critical goal of developing engaged citizens" (McBride & Mlyn, 2016, p. 4). Within the multiple pathways in higher education to social change, Schnaubelt and SchwartzCoffey (2016) asserted that students must "think about each pathway in terms of the sense of identity it confers, its language and jargon, its normative practices and hierarchies, and the power structures it requires individuals to navigate" (p. 25). The reality that different engaged approaches confer different identities, use different discourses, and normalize different power structures is of central importance to how practitioners engage undergraduates and support higher education's civic mission.

Two significant models for social change in higher education are civic engagement and social innovation, and although there are points where these two movements intersect, Schnaubelt and SchwartzCoffey (2016) suggested each comes with its own set of practices that are not always compatible. Alluding to the still developing relationship between these practices, Scobey (2015) asked whether they are more like sibling rivals or kissing cousins. This chapter engages Scobey's question by focusing on student perceptions of two specific practices within these broader approaches and ways they are sometimes in dialogue, sometimes in competition.

To better appreciate how students understand community-engaged practices, we pursued research that considers undergraduate students' perceptions of two pedagogies of engagement: service-learning and social entrepreneurship. How do our students understand the values and practices of community engagement within these two approaches? Four of the five authors of this chapter hold appointments in our university's service-learning program (our fifth author is in the Office of Assessment), so we approach this research as believers in the potential of service-learning, as critics of many of its current practices, and as outsiders to and students of social entrepreneurship education.

Our research began from our interest in understanding why social entrepreneurship was becoming so popular on our campus. In 2015, *Forbes Magazine* indicated that service-learning is among the "early building blocks of [the community engagement] movement" (Ehrlich & Fu, 2015) and described more innovative approaches being implemented on college campuses. To remain relevant among community-engaged pedagogies and at the same time retain best practices in service-learning, particularly those drawing on critical frameworks, we ask, "How can student perceptions help us understand emerging conceptualizations of community engagement in higher education?"

We have chosen to pursue this research through the lens of student perception because psychological research has explored how students' perceptions impact the learning experience, specifically how comprehension and understanding are related to existing perceptions, assumptions, and biases (Clark & Clark, 1947; Festinger, 1957; Lewin, 1938; Steele, 1988). There are specific and salient mechanisms at work in the learning process that contribute to perceptions and understandings, including implicit bias (i.e., unrecognized stereotypes), confirmation bias (i.e., making new information conform to existing biases), selective perception (i.e., perceiving what we want to when confronted with new information), and fundamental attribution error (i.e., seeing others' actions through the lens of individual factors versus larger social and systemic values) (Caverni, Fabre, & Gonzalez,

1990). While our purpose in this research was not to confirm these particular mechanisms, knowing that students' perceptions of their environment—including learning experiences and environment—significantly impact decision-making and behavior (Bandura, 1986) provides the rationale for studying student perceptions. Related to this, Mitchell and Soria (2016) investigated how student perceptions of their community-engaged experiences impact student developmental outcomes. They analyzed data from the Student Experience in the Research University (SERU) survey

> to discover how undergraduates characterized the nature of their community-based service activities at large public research universities. Students were asked to classify their service within categories including charity, public or collective action, social change, empowering others, social action, participatory democracy, and social justice. (p. 243)

Their analysis of the data suggested that when students perceived and characterized their work in the community as a form of charity, they were less likely to develop social perspective-taking, less likely to reflect on social problems, and less likely to implement social change. Mitchell and Soria concluded that student learning outcomes are influenced by student perceptions and by their characterizations of community-engaged experiences.

Our interest in researching similarities and differences in college students' perceptions of service-learning and social entrepreneurship grows out of our desire to design experiences and learning spaces that will promote a deeper understanding of and commitment to ethical engagement. Having piloted a survey of student perceptions on our campus in early 2016 (Malone, Clifford, Anderson, & Serra, 2015), we built on themes introduced by Scobey (2015) to study perceptions of these two engaged pedagogies: (a) What are the starting points for community engagement work?; (b) What attitudes about community are revealed in our forms of engagement?; (c) What are our beliefs about how social change occurs?; (d) What is the role of critical reflection in community engagement?; (e) What are perceptions about the overall effectiveness of each approach (i.e., service-learning and social entrepreneurship education)? This chapter reports and analyzes findings from a national distribution of the undergraduate student survey designed to gauge student perceptions of service-learning and social entrepreneurship, offers insights into what students think about these approaches, presents implications related to the teaching of both, and considers contemporary conditions that affect the social justice commitments of each approach.

Review of Selected Literature Comparing Service-Learning and Social Entrepreneurship Education

As chapters in this volume demonstrate, the discourses of community engagement and social entrepreneurship are significant to the practices in question. *Community engagement* and *social innovation* are umbrella terms that identify models of engagement in community; given the nature of our work, in our research we focus specifically on university student perceptions of service-learning and social entrepreneurship. In Enos's (2015) comparison of the practices, each "seeks to combine academic lessons and real world applied experiences" (p. 11). *Service-learning* is aligned with community engagement and is defined as "a teaching and learning strategy that integrates meaningful community service with instruction and reflection to enrich the learning experience, teach civic responsibility, and strengthen communities" (National Service-Learning Clearinghouse, 2001). The case for nesting social entrepreneurship under social innovation is part of its origin story (McBride & Mlyn, 2016). Social innovation is "the process of inventing, securing support for, and implementing novel solutions to social needs and problems" (Phills, Deiglmeier, & Miller, 2008, para. 1); it focuses on "new things . . . that can be an idea, a device, or a process" (McBride & Mlyn, 2016, p. 4). Social entrepreneurship is the process of pursuing innovative, sustainable solutions to social problems (Nash, 2015) with a focus on "founding enterprises" (McBride & Mlyn, 2016, p. 4).

Three organizations influence much of the narrative surrounding service-learning and social entrepreneurship education on college campuses: Campus Compact, the Carnegie Foundation for the Advancement of Teaching through its Community Engagement Classification, and Ashoka U through the Changemaker Campus Designation. These organizations communicate with campuses and faculty about forms of community engagement and support how colleges and universities design and implement pedagogies and programming. Table 4.1 presents phrases from the mission statements of each organization (or manifesto in the case of Ashoka U) indicating how individuals, community(ies), and society are positioned by the organization. These terms and phrases and their uses at the individual, community, and society levels introduce ways organizational discourses may influence faculty, staff, and student narratives about service-learning and social entrepreneurship education.

Campus Compact is the national organization most closely aligned with service-learning, while Ashoka U most closely aligns with social entrepreneurship; Carnegie's Community Engagement Classification can

TABLE 4.1
Lexicon Used by Campus Compact, the Carnegie Foundation's Community Engagement Classification, and the Ashoka U Changemaker Campus Designation

Organization	*Concepts Related to Individual*	*Concepts Related to Community*	*Concepts Related to Society*
Campus Compact	Cocreate Responsible citizenship Motivation and capacity to deliberate, act, and lead in pursuit of the public good	Health and strength of communities Communities beyond the campus—nearby and around the world Mutually respectful partnerships	Pursuit of public good Challenge to prevailing social and economic inequalities Centrality of the public purposes of higher education
Carnegie Community Engagement Classification	Collaboration Civic responsibility	Local, regional, state, national, and global communities Mutually beneficial exchange Partnership Reciprocity	Strengthen democratic values Address societal issues Contribute to public good
Ashoka U Changemaker Campus	Collaborative Changemaker Leadership Creative problem-solving Empathy	Mutually beneficial partnerships Local and global communities	Shift from traditional to more innovative Changemaking is effective organizational or societal change of any kind Social innovation

straddle both pedagogies although it is more closely referenced in community engagement and service-learning contexts. In spite of these affiliations, of note in Table 4.1 are the many commonalities in the language used to describe the practices of individuals, community, and society, including collaboration, community, and constructions of the social good. At the same time, there are hints at points of departure for the two pedagogies, such as in norms of problem-solving and suggestions of who benefits from either practice.

Hypotheses

Based on literature from the civic engagement field, we developed our hypotheses around the following themes: (a) the starting point for community engagement, (b) the attitudes toward community, (c) how change occurs, (d) the role of critical reflection on ethics and civics, and (e) the effectiveness of the approach to community (i.e., service-learning and social entrepreneurship education). We hypothesized that undergraduates would associate statements exploring each of the themes significantly with either service-learning or social entrepreneurship and that participation in either would not affect associations. We hypothesized that institutional characteristics such as Carnegie and Ashoka U classifications may matter in student perceptions of the approaches. These hypotheses rested on our belief that social entrepreneurship as a frame for community engagement is a fundamentally different practice from service-learning, with different knowledge, beliefs, attitudes, and actions corresponding to each frame. To examine these hypotheses, we proposed collecting data through an online survey of a sample of undergraduates at American universities and colleges.

Methods

The survey instrument consisted of demographic questions, open-ended definitions, Likert-type response items, and a word association task. Students rated 25 statements on a 1 to 5 Likert scale for the extent to which the statement is associated with service-learning or social entrepreneurship. The survey randomized the statement order within the 2 frameworks in order to mitigate fatigue effects for the respondents. These statements were related to the themes previously mentioned and are presented in Table 4.2. This allowed students to express that they thought each approach was equal in certain categories without comparing the approaches. The next task was a word association task in which they compared the 2 approaches, indicating that certain words such as *innovative* or *ethical* were associated more with service-learning, social entrepreneurship, or neither.

TABLE 4.2
Survey Themes and Corresponding Survey Statements

Survey Themes	*Survey Statements*
The starting point for community engagement	• Projects created by the community • The idea that the starting point of the experience is relationships • Projects created by an outsider to the community • The idea that the starting point of the experience is to solve a problem
Attitudes toward community	• Reciprocity between you and the community • Perceiving the community as your client • Perceiving the community as your partner • Creating relationships • Seeing the community as the recipient of services
How change occurs	• Humility • Developing strategies for solving a problem • Being an innovative approach to social change • Gaining its effectiveness from innovations • Being a dynamic leader in the community • Positioning you as being viewed more favorably by potential employers • Being a coworker with the community • Gaining effectiveness from the power of partnerships with the community
Role of critical reflection on ethics and civics	• Integrating critical reflection into the experience • Allocating time for all participants to reflect on the experience of community engagement • Fostering the development of civic responsibility • Being concerned with ethics of community engagement
The effectiveness of the approach to community	• University-supported participation by college students • Being a highly effective approach to addressing social problems • Being an up-to-date approach to community engagement • Making impact on societal level

Experts in service-learning and social entrepreneurshop education reviewed the tool for content and face validity. Focus groups were held with three groups of students in order to determine how students understood the questions and if questions were confusing or interpreted differently than intended. Modifications were made to the survey to improve comprehension based on student feedback. Duke University's institutional review board reviewed and approved the multisite study.

Institutional-Level Recruitment

All 48 universities that had both the Carnegie Community Engagement Classification and the Ashoka U Changemaker Campus Designation were invited to participate in the survey. Additional campuses were invited in order to attempt to include universities that fell into the following categories: R1 and R2 public and private universities from across the country.

Institutional-Level Sample and Characteristics

Ten universities agreed to participate: two R1 public universities, five R1 private universities, two R2 public universities, and one R2 private university. Six universities were in the Southeast, two in the Southwest, one in the Northeast, and one in the Midwest. All participating universities had activities that met our definitions of *service-learning* and *social entrepreneurship* although nomenclature and infrastructure varied among campuses. Nine of the universities met the Carnegie Community Engagement Classification. Four of the universities with the Carnegie Community Engagement Classification also had the Ashoka U Changemaker Campus Classification. One participating institution had neither classification.

Student Frame and Sampling Techniques at Institutions

Each institution worked with our research team to identify a sampling technique that would be feasible for the institution. Four of the institutions drew representative random samples from their undergraduate student population. Five institutions purposively sampled students enrolled in service-learning and social entrepreneurship classes and programs. One institution sent the survey to its entire undergraduate population. Across the 10 institutions, 19,186 students were invited to participate, with a mean sample size of 1,912 (SD = 2,223).

At all institutions, students were contacted by e-mail and asked to participate in the voluntary survey. The survey was administered online using the online data collection software Qualtrics (Qualtrics, Provo, UT). Informed consent was obtained at the start of the survey. A $5 donation to the United Way was offered for the first 200 completed surveys.

Students were asked to disclose their gender identity, ethnicity, first-generation status, and previous involvement with service-learning and social entrepreneurship.

Student Sample and Response Rate

There were 1,136 respondents to the survey. This resulted in an overall response rate of 5.92% and varied by institution from 2.56% to 27.03%. Data cleaning revealed that 121 respondents did not provide answers beyond the demographic data questions. Those surveys were eliminated, reducing the number of students included in the final data set to 1,015.

Demographics and Experiences of Sample

Of the 1,015 student respondents, 72% (n = 729) identified as female, 27% (n = 274) as male, and 1% as nonbinary. Sixty-six percent (n = 673) of our sample identified as White, 17% (n = 167) as Asian, 7% (n = 66) as Black, and 9% (n = 93) as other races. Seventeen percent (n = 168) were in their first year of university, 26% (n = 261) in their second, 31% (n = 318) in their third, 19% (n = 192) in their fourth, and 6% (n = 57) in their fifth or more. Eleven percent (n = 110) were first-generation college students.

Seventy-three percent (n = 686) of respondents had some personal experience with service-learning compared to only 21% (n = 209) reporting personal experience with social entrepreneurship. Ten percent (n = 102) were not sure if they had a service-learning experience, and 20% (n = 197) were not sure if they had an experience with social entrepreneurship. Of the students could identify specific experiences with service-learning, 39% (n = 189) reported having 1 experience, 30% (n = 142) reported having 2 experiences, and 31% (n = 151) reported having 3 or more experiences. Of the students who could identify specific social entrepreneurship experiences, 45% (n = 47) reported having one experience, 22% (n = 23) reported having two experiences, and 33% (n = 34) reported having three or more experiences.

Data Analysis

We tested each statement association for the two approaches using a t test comparing mean responses from all respondents for service-learning and social entrepreneurship question sets. We further examined how perceptions of students who attended institutions possessing both Carnegie and Ashoka U classifications might differ from those of students who attended

TABLE 4.3
Respondents' Previous Experience and Institutional Affiliation

	Reported Service-Learning Experience (n)	*Reported Social Entrepreneurship Experience (n)*	*Reported Experiences With Both Service-Learning and Social Entrepreneurship (n)*	*Unsure of Previous Participation (n)*
Classified as both Carnegie and Ashoka	566	185	105	102
Not classified as both Carnegie and Ashoka	246	25	14	197

institutions that did not possess both classifications by running similar tests for each group and comparing the results. Significance was defined as $p < .05$ for all tests. Table 4.3 provides a breakdown of respondents' backgrounds and institutional associations.

Findings

We asked students to define in their own words both *service-learning* and *social entrepreneurship* in order to gauge their knowledge and understanding of the approaches before they responded to any survey items. The students varied greatly in their ability to define the approaches. For the *service-learning framework*, 87.5% of the sample provided a definition but 12.5% either actively said they could not define the term or left the question blank. For the *social entrepreneurship framework*, 68.5% of the sample defined the term but 31.5% actively indicated that they did not know the definition or left the question blank. For schools that did not have both Carnegie Community Engagement Classification and Ashoka U Changemaker Campus Classification in the sample, the percentage of students saying they did not know the definitions or choosing not to answer the question rose to 41.6%.

Word clouds were created to get a better sense of the types of language used by respondents when defining *service-learning* and

Figure 4.1. Word clouds of student-constructed definitions.

social entrepreneurship. For the word clouds in Figure 4.1, *service, learning, service-learning, social*, and *entrepreneurship* were removed in order to facilitate clarity of presentation.

Responses of students who participated in one or more service-learning experiences were compared to responses of students who participated in one or more social entrepreneurship experiences. Doing so offers insight into participants' perceptions of service-learning and social entrepreneurship, specifically how these perceptions might overlap between groups and whether these groups shared similar perspectives on the nature of these two approaches. Our findings indicated that regardless of previous experience with service-learning and social entrepreneurship, participants shared very similar views of these two approaches, specifically the ways in which service-learning and social entrepreneurship differ. Tests for significance showed matching associations between the service-learning participants and the social entrepreneurship participants for 18 of 25 statements. Table 4.4 presents the 18 statements, which had both a significant difference ($p < .05$) between approaches and matching associations between the service-learning and social entrepreneurship groups.

Seven of 25 statements were not significantly associated with either approach. Of these 7 statements, both groups associated 5 of them with the service-learning approach, although the difference within the social entrepreneurship group was not significant ($p > .05$). Both groups associated one of the other remaining statements with social entrepreneurship, but the results from the social entrepreneurship group were not significant ($p > .05$). The final remaining statement showed different associated approaches for each group, and, once again, the differences between the

TABLE 4.4
Statements That All Students Significantly Associated With Service-Learning or Social Entrepreneurship

Survey Theme	*Statements Associated With Service-Learning*	*Statements Associated With Social Entrepreneurship*
The starting point for community engagement	• Projects created by the community • The idea that the starting point of the experience is relationships	• Projects created by an outsider to the community • The idea that the starting point of the experience is to solve a problem
Attitudes toward community	• Reciprocity between you and the community	• Perceiving the community as your client
How change occurs	• Humility	• Developing strategies for solving a problem • Being an innovative approach to social change • Gaining its effectiveness from innovations • Being a dynamic leader in the community • Positioning you as being viewed more favorably by potential employers
Role of critical reflection on ethics and civics	• Integrating critical reflection into the experience • Allocating time for all participants to reflect on the experience of community engagement	
The effectiveness of the approach to community	• University-supported participation by college students	• Being a highly effective approach to addressing social problems • Being an up-to-date approach to community engagement • Making impact on societal level

$p < .05$.

approaches for the social entrepreneurship group were not significant ($p > .05$). Table 4.5 shows the seven statements for which the service-learning and social entrepreneurship participants did not share a clear agreement on the ways these approaches differ.

Associations of the 25 statements to either the service-learning or social entrepreneurship approach were also explored based on respondents' institution type. Respondents were grouped into 2 categories based on whether an institution had both the Carnegie and Ashoka U classifications. Student responses from the four institutions that did have both classifications were compared to student responses from all other institutions. Tests for significance showed matching associations between the Carnegie-and-Ashoka U group and the other institutions for 20 of 25 statements. Table 4.6 presents the 20 statements that had both a significant difference ($p < .05$) between approaches and matching associations between the Carnegie-and-Ashoka U group and the other institutions.

Findings were less clear for the remaining 5 of 25 statements. Of these statements both groups associated four of them with the social entrepreneurship approach, although the difference within the 6 institutions that were not Carnegie-and-Ashoka U classified was not significant ($p > .05$). For the remaining statement, both groups associated it with

TABLE 4.5
Statements Not Significantly Associated With Service-Learning or Social Entrepreneurship by All Students

Survey Statements	*Statement Associations*
• Perceiving the community as your partner • Being a coworker with the community • Creating relationships • Fostering the development of civic responsibility • Being concerned with ethics of community engagement	Shared association with service-learning but difference was not significant for both groups ($p > .05$)
• Seeing the community as the recipient of services	Shared association with social entrepreneurship but difference was not significant for both groups ($p > .05$)
• Gaining its effectiveness from the power of partnerships with the community	Mixed perception but difference was not significant for both groups ($p > .05$)

TABLE 4.6
Statements That Students Significantly Associated With Service-Learning or Social Entrepreneurship at Carnegie–and–Ashoka U Institutions and Other Institutions

Survey Theme	*Statements Associated With Service-Learning*	*Statements Associated With Social Entrepreneurship*
The starting point for community engagement	• Projects created by the community • The idea that the starting point of the experience is relationships	• Projects created by an outsider to the community • The idea that the starting point of the experience is to solve a problem
Attitudes toward community	• Perceiving the community as your partner • Creating relationships • Reciprocity between you and the community	• Perceiving the community as your client
How change occurs	• Being a coworker with the community • Humility	• Developing strategies for solving a problem • Being an innovative approach to social change • Gaining its effectiveness from innovations • Being a dynamic leader in the community • Positioning you as being viewed more favorably by potential employers
Role of critical reflection on ethics and civics	• Integrating critical reflection into the experience • Fostering the development of civic responsibility • Being concerned with ethics of community engagement • Allocating time for all participants to reflect on the experience of community engagement	
The effectiveness of the approach to community	• University-supported participation by college students	

$p < .05$

service-learning, but, again, the results from the Carnegie-and-Ashoka U group were not significant ($p > .05$). Table 4.7 shows the five statements for which the Carnegie-and-Ashoka U group and the other group did not share a clear agreement on the ways these approaches differ.

Respondents were also asked to associate a single word or phrase with service-learning, social entrepreneurship, or neither approach. Responses to the single-word or single-phrase associations mirror the findings of the 25 statements shared in Tables 4.4 through 4.7. Respondents more frequently associated words and phrases such as *innovative*, *taking charge*, *cutting edge*, and *solving a problem* with social entrepreneurship. Respondents more frequently associated words and phrases such as *community-focused*, *humility*, *civic responsibility*, *engaged*, and *moral* with service-learning. Table 4.8 provides the overall responses for the 20 words and phrases. The words most highly associated with service-learning are presented in descending order, and the words most highly associated with social entrepreneurship appear in ascending order.

An examination of the data revealed that regardless of whether students had more experience with service-learning or with social entrepreneurship, both service-learning students and social entrepreneurship students agreed that the two approaches are different and that the differences are distinguishable. The data also revealed that regardless of whether an institution of higher education has both, one, or none of the classifications of Carnegie Community Engagement and Ashoka U Changemaker Campus, once again both groups of students agreed that the two approaches are different and that the differences are distinguishable.

TABLE 4.7
Statements Not Significantly Associated by Students in Carnegie-and-Ashoka U Institutions or Other Institutions

Survey Statements	*Statement Associations*
• Gaining its effectiveness from the power of partnerships with the community	Shared association with service-learning but difference was not significant for both groups ($p > .05$)
• Seeing the community as the recipient of services • Being a highly effective approach to addressing social problems • Being an up-to-date approach to community engagement • Making impact on societal level	Shared association with social entrepreneurship but difference was not significant for both groups ($p > .05$)

TABLE 4.8
Word Associations

	Service-Learning (%)	*Social Entrepreneurship (%)*	*Neither (%)*
Community-focused	77	20	3
Humility (humble)	76	10	14
Engaged	72	25	3
Civic responsibility (civically responsible)	72	23	5
Moral	70	18	12
Ethical	64	25	11
Mutually beneficial	62	31	7
Collaborative	61	35	4
Inclusive	55	23	22
Heroic	46	21	33
Social activist	44	47	9
Savior	32	24	45
Privileged	35	40	25
Self-focused	23	46	32
Political	17	56	27
Exciting	32	58	10
Solving a problem	21	73	6
Taking charge	11	79	10
Cutting edge	6	79	15
Innovative	9	85	5

Students tended to characterize service-learning as an approach that is associated with a focus on community and relationships, ethical collaboration, humility, and critical reflection. Students did not strongly associate service-learning with taking charge or being innovative, cutting edge, up to date, political, and highly effective in addressing social problems. Students tended to characterize social entrepreneurship as an approach associated with being innovative, cutting edge, and exciting; taking charge; starting off with solving a problem; involving dynamic leadership; and making an impact on a societal level. Students did not strongly associate social entrepreneurship with being humble, moral, community-focused, and civically responsible and involving critical reflection.

Despite what we might find in the literature and what we learn in conversations with fellow community-engaged practitioners, students in our sample did not have particularly strong associations with characteristics such as being heroic, a savior, privileged, or self-focused for either service-learning or social entrepreneurship. Interestingly, although the associations were not particularly robust, students did rate service-learning as more "heroic" than social entrepreneurship and social entrepreneurship as more "self-focused" than service-learning.

Study Limitations

This study, which was exploratory in nature, examined the perceptions of service-learning and social entrepreneurship across multiple institutions. Despite this being the only quantitative investigation to our knowledge of student perceptions of service-learning and social entrepreneurship, there are several limitations that affect the generalizability of our study.

Institutional selection, although representing a range of institutional types, was based on the institution's ability and willingness to participate rather than meeting specific criteria. Recruitment for the study varied among institutions in both the size and targeted student populations but heavily relied on purposive sampling of students already invested in service-learning or social entrepreneurship. Because of smaller response rates at some institutions, we analyzed institutional-level data only in aggregate and with respect to Ashoka U and Carnegie classifications. Students who participated self-selected to fill out the survey. While the results of this study may inform the larger discussion about the nature of service-learning and social entrepreneurship, it is important to acknowledge the variation among and even within institutions. Within institutions, we were not able to control for differences in implementations of these approaches from course to course and instructor to instructor—not only between courses identified as service-learning or social entrepreneurship but also within the specific service-learning or social entrepreneurship departments. These differences may impact student perceptions of the fields and their responses to the survey used in this study. Despite these limitations, we feel the data are unique in their scope and ability to speak to multiple institutions' students' perceptions of these two fields.

Discussion

What did we learn from surveying 1,015 college students with previous experiences with either service-learning or social entrepreneurship from differently classified institutions? How can we strengthen our practice by analyzing the ways students define these two approaches in their own words, respond to 25 Likert statements about each practice, and complete a 20-item word association task? What are the possible implications of our research for both theory and practice of community-engaged pedagogy? To address these questions we place our findings in conversation with the following areas of scholarship that are relevant to the field of community engagement: (a) scholarship on teaching, learning, and student development and (b) scholarship on social justice in engaged pedagogies.

Service-Learning, Social Entrepreneurship, and Student Development

We accept—as most, if not all, of the contributors to this volume do—that higher education has at its core a civic mission, a mission to fully develop within students a sense of civic identity and engaged citizenship. This mission is essentially one of human development—and in the context of higher education our efforts often focus on multiple areas of student development, such as academic, intellectual, ethical, social, identity, career, and civic. Colleges and universities exist for several purposes, but central among them is the holistic development of their students. If we accept the premise that students' prior knowledge and existing beliefs shape potential new understandings, there appears to be a number of ways that current cognitive developmental theory and constructivist perspectives on learning can inform our community-engaged pedagogies. For one, it seems essential that we make more visible what students already know, what they believe, and what they see as being the undergirding values and principles of the community-engaged pedagogies we are using to teach them in our classrooms and community-based experiences.

We assert that the findings from our research provide insight into college student development that has implications for how we best use service-learning and social entrepreneurship as engaged pedagogies. An examination of the data from the task asking students to construct definitions of *service-learning* and *social entrepreneurship* revealed that students for the most part come to their community-engaged learning experiences with varying levels of understanding of these two approaches. In our sample only 12.5% of students indicated they did not know how to define *service-learning* or left that question blank. In contrast, 31.5% of students indicated that they did not know how to define *social entrepreneurship* or declined to answer. It appears that many students possess at least some knowledge about service-learning, whereas fewer students appear to be familiar with social entrepreneurship.

When considering, for example, how students characterized the starting point for community engagement for each practice, students made associations consistent with literature in the field: The perception that the starting point for community engagement is to solve a problem was significantly associated with social entrepreneurship, while the perception that the starting point for community engagement is relationship(s) was significantly associated with service-learning. This is true for all students surveyed: those at Carnegie Community Engagement Classification schools, at Ashoka U Changemaker Campus schools, and the school with neither designation. When considering perceptions about how change occurs in communities, once again students made clear associations that reflect literature in each field: Developing strategies for solving a problem and being an innovative approach to social change were associated with social entrepreneurship, while being a coworker with the community was associated with service-learning. Again, these perceptions were statistically significant for all students, with students attending Carnegie– and Ashoka U–classified universities (i.e., campuses invested enough to seek classification) adding coworking with community as the way change happens via service-learning. In spite of Enos's (2015) warning to avoid an oversimplification "that service-learning develops empathetic citizens while social entrepreneurship education creates students who possess problem-solving skills" (p. 67), definitions in the field and findings in our research suggest that this is exactly what is happening.

Results from the word association task indicate that students have clear associations about attributes for both service-learning and social entrepreneurship. Literature in each field suggests the type of individual each practice seeks to cultivate, with social entrepreneurship seeking bold, creative, and driven individuals (Bornstein, 2007) and service-learning seeking students who are more tolerant, altruistic, and collaborative (Mitchell, 2008). With few exceptions, our initial hypotheses about associations students would make for each practice were borne out in the word association question on our survey.

Prior to administering the survey, we anticipated that more students would characterize social entrepreneurship as heroic, but as the results indicated, there was a stronger association of heroism with service-learning (46% for service-learning versus 21% for social entrepreneurship).

Anticipating that several of the terms would have no clear association, we underestimated the extent to which students perceived service-learning to be engaged (72% for service-learning versus 25% for social entrepreneurship) and social entrepreneurship to be political (17% for service-learning versus 56% for social entrepreneurship) (see Table 4.8). Seeing associations at 70% or higher indicates that students have clear perceptions about certain attributes of each approach. Our intention is not to reify attributes of either practice but, rather, to show the strength of students' perceptions and the extent to which we may trace these perceptions to literature in the field as well as perhaps our own teaching practices.

Our interpretation of these data suggests that our teaching in these fields may work to reinforce existing schema and students' stereotypical perceptions as opposed to help students create more nuanced and complex understandings. However, our research also points to the possibilities of introducing students to more complicated and cultivated understandings of each practice. In examining the word clouds created from student definitions of social entrepreneurship and service-learning, for example, our first attempt to visualize definitions revealed a not-too-surprising tendency to offer circular definitions such that the words that stand out were those embedded in the definition (i.e., service, learning, social, entrepreneurship).

By removing the terms that comprise the concept, the resulting word clouds (see Figure 4.1) offer faculty in either—or both—fields the opportunity to consider students' existing understandings of these practices as a starting point for building greater complexity. We could construct a sentence from the words that jump out after removing self-referential terms to suggest that students understand service-learning as *students learn[ing] knowledge [by] work[ing with] others*. In addition to these primary associations are words that can facilitate more critical thinking about service-learning, such as *giving, need, real,* and *benefit*, or, diving deeper, we see *hands, impact,* and *time*. Applying the same method to student-offered definitions of social entrepreneurship suggests students understand it as *new ideas [and] solutions [for] issues [in] society*. Other points of entry come from words such as *help, better*, and *profit*, or, drilling deeper, we see *private, market*, and *mission*.

It is clear that students in our sample have knowledge and beliefs about service-learning and social entrepreneurship. However, students' existing knowledge is not necessarily accurate or good knowledge. As Thompson (2013) and others have pointed out, these prior beliefs and knowledge can be facilitating or they can interfere with new learning. The implication for practitioners is that we must be intentional in our efforts to expose students' perceptions of the ways we approach community engagement and at the same time create space for them to explore and articulate their own goals for engagement. We must think strategically about how to work closely with our students as they construct deeper and more nuanced understandings of their community-engaged experiences. We also must recognize that high-quality practice must involve community partners as coeducators in exposing students' perceptions—interrupting and disrupting ideas and behaviors that need to be challenged.

Though it may seem reassuring that our students appear to come to their community-engaged learning experiences with commonly shared ideas about the differences between service-learning and social entrepreneurship, these shared perceptions become more problematic when we begin to interrogate them. For example, if our students indeed perceive social entrepreneurship as not valuing critical reflection, this is a notion that we as teachers must challenge. If our students perceive social entrepreneurship and service-learning as having different ethical values, then as practitioners we need to provide more and deeper opportunities for students to explore the ethics of each approach both in the classroom and in the context of their engagement with communities. It may be of benefit to bring together service-learning students and social entrepreneurship students who are working in the same neighborhoods or who are addressing the same social problem. Collaborative reflection sessions might help each group of students grow and develop in new ways.

The words that students in our sample associated with service-learning and with social entrepreneurship also provide opportunities for us as educators to help students develop more complex ways of thinking about community engagement. For example, if students no longer see service-learning as an "exciting" or a "cutting-edge" approach to community engagement, in what ways might this be problematic for us as teachers of service-learning classes? If our students enter our classrooms with the perception that social entrepreneurship is an approach that requires "taking charge," what are the implications for teaching students who might, as numerous scholars have proposed, see taking charge as suggesting a masculine-oriented space and norms (Gomez & Korine, 2008; Jones, 2014; Peredo & Chrisman, 2006; Tedmanson, Verduyn, Essers, & Gartner, 2012)? These are but a few examples of the ways that often unexamined perceptions, values, and beliefs that our students bring to our community-engaged classes might shape their understandings.

There is much insight practitioners in the field of community-engaged learning can gain from putting our work into conversation with the scholarship of teaching and learning. By connecting our work in community-engaged pedagogies to the principles of learning, teaching, and student development that have been identified within the scholarship of teaching and learning, we better inform our own work and learn how we as community engagement practitioners might more effectively address the question of how to best foster the holistic development of engaged citizens.

Service-Learning, Social Entrepreneurship, and Social Justice

If there is general agreement that higher education has at its core a civic mission, less certain is the extent to which higher education embraces a social justice mission. We adopt Mitchell's (2010) description of the potential of a social justice framework, in this case focused on service-learning:

> I believe in a service-learning pedagogy focused on social justice aims that challenges and changes the systems and structures that create inequality and perpetuate injustice, and that asks students to examine their biases and assumptions, to acknowledge privilege, and to open their minds and hearts to a new possibility for themselves and the world. (p. 97)

This is a tall order for many service-learning courses and instructors. Through the social justice lens, it is not enough to arrange service experiences that "help" the community without also challenging the individual practices and social systems that create or perpetuate unjust conditions. Operationally, new possibilities for self and the world and more equitable distribution of resources may push at many taken-for-granted, if fragile, social contracts, many of which involve relationships between institutions of higher education and communities. Cipolle (2010) argued that service-learning has the potential to nurture "social-justice citizens" who "[become] committed to service . . . , committed to social justice, and [develop] a critical consciousness" (p. 11), although this is by no means a certain outcome. Cipolle borrowed from models of White identity development to suggest movement from initial to emergent to developing to maturing stages when cultivating critical consciousness among students. Her method is to move students from charity to caring and from caring to social justice, facilitating students' "reflect[ion] on targets and agents of multiple systems of oppression (racism, sexism, classism, ageism, heterosexism, and others) and examin[ation of] what they can do to combat oppression" (p. 14).

If Cipolle's model is difficult in service-learning despite the emergence of social justice framing in the field, it is perhaps a greater challenge in social entrepreneurship education, given the limited foothold social justice has in *that* field. As early as 2007, Thekaekara and Thekaekara described the challenges social entrepreneurship faces about social justice:

> Social Entrepreneurship is an idea whose time has come—it is in keeping with the twenty-first century, where economics has overtaken politics. Social activists of the 70's have to recognize this. On the other hand the more modern apolitical approaches to poverty rooted in business models have to recognize that creation of wealth even if it is for the poor is not enough. It has to be accompanied by the creation of power. Economic improvement has to go with political empowerment. . . . In order to do this we have to be more careful in applying the term social entrepreneurship. (p. 10)

It is much more likely to see so-called traditional models of service-learning and social entrepreneurship in higher education, those that "[emphasize] service without attention to systems of inequality" (Mitchell, 2008, p. 50), than more critical social justice practices and orientations. Mitchell argued that moving beyond these traditional practices requires a critical service-learning orientation, one that is "unapologetic in its aim to dismantle structures of injustice" (p. 50). Critical service-learning demands a new framework: a social change orientation working to redistribute power and developing authentic relationships.

Our findings, however, reflect a strong degree of continuity from more traditional—some might argue normative—literature of each field to student perceptions of service-learning and social entrepreneurship. This can be seen in the word associations highlighted in Table 4.8, for example, where service-learning is associated with relationship (i.e., humility, collaborative, civic responsibility) while associations with social entrepreneurship focus on the impact or action of the approach (i.e., innovative, solving a problem, cutting edge). While there were limited choices among the more critical words and concepts we presented to students in our survey, it is interesting that the most even split in word associations was for social activist, associated with service-learning at 44% and with social entrepreneurship at 47%. Given the opportunity to query these respondents, it would be worthwhile to understand their definitions of *social activist* and the extent to which those definitions align with critical practices.

Sally Jones (2014) has been an influential critical voice in entrepreneurship education. Her work with colleagues (Farney, Frederiksen, Hannibal, & Jones, 2016) established a description of more traditional forms of social entrepreneurship education:

> Entrepreneurship education in higher education aims to transform students' attitudes, values, and self-understandings (Holmgren and From 2005), creating an imperative for *all* students to become enterprising (Pittaway and Cope 2007). This transformation manifests as an increased focus on the entrepreneur as a person, identified by certain abilities and practices, which should be stimulated and trained. Hence, the entrepreneur stands out as a driving identity in the new economy, which more individuals are encouraged to take up (Lewis and Llewellyn 2004). (Jones, 2014, p. 516)

In this description we see the focus on the individual in development of student entrepreneurs, with the suggestion that all students should be enterprising. This is echoed in Ashoka U's manifesto that everyone is a changemaker (see Table 4.1); however, Ashoka U also includes collaboration as a strategy for individual changemakers. Jones's work is also central to critiques of traditional practices in social entrepreneurship education:

> As a totalizing discourse, the hidden curriculum of [entrepreneurship education] instills taken-for-granted notions about entrepreneurship as a universal and intrinsic good, which will lead to salvation and the promised land of individual and national success, wealth and status for the chosen. This makes it difficult, if not impossible, to question why entrepreneurship is to be promoted. (p. 13)

Again we see the focus on the individual's success, with Scobey's (2015) description of the social entrepreneur's hutzpah elevated to field-based assumptions of "universal and intrinsic good" along with "individual wealth and status."

The work of scholars such as Mitchell and Jones challenges us to take a hard look at traditional models of service-learning and social entrepreneurship and consider what practices normalize traditional constructions of student, university, faculty, or community; what practices facilitate construction of the academy as an asset and the community as a deficit; and what practices imagine undergraduate service-learning students as collaborative and undergraduate social entrepreneur students as driven. To continue these traditional associations, and to consider their construction, we can return to the discourses that Campus Compact, the Carnegie Community Engagement Classification, and the Ashoka U Changemaker Campus Designation use to frame perceptions in the fields of service-learning and social entrepreneurship. Putting the terms used by these three organizations in conversation with the 25 Likert statements students rated according to their association of the statement with each pedagogy (see Tables 4.6 and 4.7) highlights the power of these organizations' discursive positioning of the individual, the community, and society in relation to pedagogies of engagement.

Campus Compact, the organization most closely aligned with service-learning, positions the individual as a cocreator with community and invested in the public good. These associations are visible in our survey results given the way students see relationship and reciprocity as characteristics of service-learning. Ashoka U, the organization more closely aligned with social entrepreneurship, positions the individual as a leader focused on creative problem-solving, mirrored in our research by student associations of problem-solving by outsiders to the community (or client) with social entrepreneurship. Per the definition by Jones and her colleagues that we cited, the individual is the primary unit of analysis in social entrepreneurship education, an idea amplified in Bornstein's (2007) description of the entrepreneur in *How to Change the World: Social Entrepreneurs and the Power of New Ideas*:

> Above all, this book shows that it takes creative individuals with fixed determination and indomitable will to propel the innovation that society needs to tackle its toughest problems. It shows that an important social change frequently begins with a single entrepreneurial author: one obsessive individual who sees a problem and envisions a new solution, who takes the initiative to act on that vision, who gathers resources and builds organizations to protect and market that vision, who provides the energy and sustained focus to overcome the inevitable resistance. (p. 3)

Given such definitions, it is easy to see how undergraduates' perceptions of social entrepreneurship identity are discursively constructed; these concepts show up in news headlines, on university websites, and in our research.

Both service-learning and social entrepreneurship reference the shifting locus of control between the individual and society. In service-learning, Cipolle (2010) argues that constructive service-learning experiences require thoughtful critical reflection to move students to consider "institutional, systemic view[s] of the causes of injustice and inequality" (p. 11), moving, then, from the individual to society. Cipolle goes on to lift up the possibilities of service-learning to move from individual acts of charity that may perpetuate the status quo to an understanding of service-learning as an act that co-occurs with community and requires students' reflection on "multiple systems of oppression" (p. 14). Critical reflection, then, is offered as the strategy that facilitates movement from individual to public good. In social entrepreneurship, Giridharadas (2011) offers a definition of *social entrepreneurship* that suggests some of the barriers to integration of social justice in social entrepreneurship:

> Earnest problem-solving elites devote themselves to social causes, using the ethos and methods of business. . . . Social entrepreneurs tend to believe that problems can be solved to the benefit of all. In their ideal world, money makers make their money, the poor are rescued from poverty, elites find meaning, and governments are circumvented.

The social entrepreneur student is not asked to be reflective in this culture of "everyone wins." There is realization of public good ("the poor are rescued from poverty") but not without individual gain in the forms of money and meaning.

As we have discussed, these narratives are present on campus and clearly shape how students form their perceptions of the different frameworks. And yet, it is also essential to underscore that the idealized model of community engagement is not always reflected in the on-the-ground reality that students come to know. The real interactions in service-learning and social entrepreneurship courses, as well as the backgrounds of the students, will impact how the students perceive the experience. The critical service-learning literature, for example, challenges us to refuse complacency in the face of "helping" and "fixing" models of service-learning and to engage in reflection and critical thinking on practices and potential outcomes so that we are pushed to adopt goals of social justice in the work we do. Although all practitioners in the field do not embrace social justice service-learning, it is fair to say that it has firmer footing than does social justice in social entrepreneurship education. Moreover, as is demonstrated in this chapter's discussion of the relationships between service-learning and social entrepreneurship, we invite social entrepreneurship educators to consider the field's commitments to social justice and the practices that may facilitate those commitments.

We recognize the introduction of social justice as a contested space in higher education, connected to purposes of education and beliefs about social change. Although perhaps a strange bedfellow for proponents of community engagement to reference, Stanley Fish (2009) noted a challenge to social entrepreneurship:

> The objection (which I am reporting, not making) is that in the passage from a state in which actions are guided by an overarching notion of the public good to a state in which individual entrepreneurs "freely" pursue their private goods, values like morality, justice, fairness, empathy, nobility and love are either abandoned or redefined in market terms.

Of significance for both service-learning and social entrepreneurship is the larger national context in which both practices, as well as higher education generally, operate: a culture that seems to straddle values of neoconservatism *and* neoliberalism with real consequences for millennial students in higher education. Slaughter and Rhodes (2009) claimed that neoliberalism pushed higher education to shift from a "public good regime . . . to an academic capitalism knowledge/learning regime [that] values knowledge privatization and profit taking" (p. 29) over public interests. In addition, Raddon and Harrison (2015) stated that "neo-liberal subjects are driven to emulate business entities by becoming more personally innovative, entrepreneurial, and efficient even in areas of life where markets do not operate" (p. 138). To this picture, neoconservatism adds a prodemocracy focus on U.S. interests and distrust of any radical—or critical—ideologies.

It is the allure of the market and promises of profit that raise questions about the possibility of social justice social entrepreneurship. Can both aspirations—for justice and for entrepreneurship—coexist? This is not to suggest that service-learning has reconciled this challenge, particularly in the neoliberal moment that values an individual for contributions to the workforce and the position of the United States in global markets. Neoliberalism leaves social justice service vulnerable to taking responsibility for larger and larger shares of the social safety net while also opening service to critique for propping up unproductive and underproductive contributors to the U.S. economy. It is worth noting, however, that the term *political* is associated with social entrepreneurship in our study (56% compared to 17% for service-learning). This finding is difficult to interpret because we are uncertain as to how students connect *political* with tools for social change within democratic engagement. One possible interpretation is that because students perceived social entrepreneurship as more change oriented (see Table 4.6), they associated dynamic action with being *political*. This needs a deeper investigation in order to understand better how service-learning and social entrepreneurship lead to the development of lifelong democratic skills, such as social activism and active citizenship.

Implications

Our study seeks to build on efforts to better understand the role played by students' perceptions and characterizations of their community-based learning experiences—and the implications of students' existing beliefs about service-learning and social entrepreneurship for faculty who use these particular approaches. Developing an understanding of students' perceptions is important because current research suggests, for example, that we must expose and confront service as charity perceptions and orientations if we wish to have a transformative impact on our students (Stewart & Webster, 2011). As Stewart and Webster argue, when scholars and practitioners understand how students see and think about community engagement, they are able to shape theory and practice to disrupt inaccurate assumptions and to create more impactful educative experiences.

Our research has led us to develop a set of practical implications for faculty in higher education who seek to use service-learning and/or social entrepreneurship as transformative pedagogies. These implications include our need as practitioners to recognize that students are not blank slates. Educators who utilize community-engaged pedagogies, such as service-learning and social entrepreneurship, need to understand that existing beliefs and perceptions matter. The ways students see and characterize their community engagement experiences impact how they approach and what they take away from those experiences. Grenfell (2004) asserted that the existence of an imagined student in our classroom can result in faculty members ignoring "the way that the [real student] sees the world" (p. 78). This failure on the part of the educators to make visible in intentional ways the prior knowledge, beliefs, and perceptions of their students creates barriers to transformative learning.

However, it is not sufficient just to be aware that students bring prior knowledge into the classroom. We must make that knowledge visible. Effective instruction involves the activation of schema, which is the intentional use of pedagogical strategies to have students bring into their current awareness what they already know and believe. This includes ways to interrogate and fully expose students' current beliefs and perceptions. Once students begin to recognize and articulate their beliefs about community engagement, we must interrogate their beliefs deeply through reflection, social interaction, and peer analysis. This critical reflection process grounds our exploration and problematizing of community engagement. One aspect of "troubling" students' characterizations of service-learning and social entrepreneurship is our need to disrupt stereotypical thinking by directly addressing issues of power differential, privilege, and doing to versus being with community. As practitioners, we need to establish critical consciousness as a desired learning outcome.

By designing opportunities for perspective-taking, we expose students to new ways of thinking about the world. We need to use multiple approaches to critical reflection that place students in situations in which they begin to see the world through the eyes of others. As Piaget (1967) asserted, effective teachers create situations that allow students to suspend their own point of view while taking alternate points of view. Perspective-taking can facilitate in-group/out-group understanding and expand students' critical consciousness. Because students often conflate perspective-taking with empathy (Galinsky, Maddux, Gilin, & White, 2008), we want to underscore the importance of examining the role of empathy. Perspective-taking is primarily a cognitive activity that may or may not lead to the development of empathy. Empathy often takes the form of an emotional response. As practitioners we need to provide space for students' emotions in their community-engaged learning experiences.

Finally, we need to direct attention to how we challenge students' epistemic beliefs. Intellectual and ethical development in the college years can be fostered when we make explicit to our students their implicit views of knowledge (Baxter Magolda, 1992). When we challenge students' epistemic beliefs by asking them where knowledge comes from and how we come to know things, we increase their capacity to think critically. We foster their development by moving students along the continuum of knowledge as an absolute to more nuanced ways of thinking that allow for shades of meaning. The role of community partners as coeducators creates opportunities for students to receive varied points of view and decenters academia as the creator of knowledge. Community partners may help expose students' perceptions and serve as coeducators in interrupting beliefs that need to be challenged. This generative process needs to be nurtured. As practitioners, we need to lessen our students' need for cognitive closure and simple answers. Service-learning and social entrepreneurship have enormous potential to move students from lower levels of epistemological beliefs that are dualistic (Perry, 1970), absolute (Baxter Magolda, 1992), silently received knowledge (Belenky, Clinchy, Goldberg, & Tarule, 1986), and judgmental (King & Kitchner, 1994).

As pedagogical approaches, service-learning and social entrepreneurship are both built on the fundamental principle that, as Dewey (1938/1977) indicated, "education is essentially a social process" (p. 65). Faculty have the responsibility to intentionally describe and orient students to the different approaches, and yet, it is through social interaction, collaborative learning, and the building of learning communities that students and faculty gain capacity to disclose and confront their beliefs, values, and unexamined perceptions. Both service-learning and social entrepreneurship provide opportunities for cohort-based experiences in which participants share a sense of belonging to a community of learning. By fully embracing the social dimension of the learning process, these two ascendant approaches to community engagement can begin to realize their full potential.

References

Bandura, A. (1986). *Social foundations of thought and action: A social cognitive theory*. Englewood Cliffs, NJ: Prentice Hall.

Baxter Magolda, M. (1992). *Knowing and reasoning in college: Gender-related patterns in students' intellectual development* San Francisco, CA: Jossey-Bass.

Belenky, M. F., Clinchy, B. M., Goldberg, N. R., & Tarule, J. M. (1986). *Women's ways of knowing: The development of self, voice, and mind*. New York, NY: Basic Books.

Bornstein, D. (2007). *How to change the world: Social entrepreneurs and the power of new ideas*. Oxford, UK: Oxford University Press.

Caverni, J. P., Fabre, J. M., & Gonzalez, M. (1990). *Cognitive biases*. New York, NY: Elsevier Science.

Cipolle, S. B. (2010). *Service-learning and social justice: Engaging students in social change*. Lanham, MD: Rowman & Littlefield.

Clark, K. B., & Clark, M. P. (1947). Racial identification and preference among Negro children. In E. L. Hartley (Ed.), *Readings in social psychology* (pp. 169–178). New York, NY: Holt, Rinehart and Winston.

Dewey, J. (1997). *Experience and education*. New York: Free Press. (Original work published 1938)

Ehrlich, T., & Fu, E. (2015, October 7). Universities power up for public service. *Forbes*. Retrieved from https://www.forbes.com/sites/ehrlichfu/2015/10/07/universities-power-up-for-public-service/#44c63f8360b1

Enos, S. (2015). *Service-learning and social entrepreneurship in higher education: A pedagogy of social change*. New York, NY: Palgrave Macmillan.

Farney, S., Frederiksen, S. H., Hannibal, M., & Jones, S. (2016). A CULTure of entrepreneurship education. *Entrepreneurship & Regional Development, 28*(7–8), 514–535. doi:10.1080/08985626.2016.1221228

Festinger, L. (1957). *A theory of cognitive dissonance*. Palo Alto, CA: Stanford University Press.

Fish, S. (2009, March 8). Neoliberalism and higher education. *New York Times*. Retrieved from https://opinionator.blogs.nytimes.com/2009/03/08/neoliberalism-and-higher-education/

Galinsky, A. D., Maddux, W. W., Gilin, D., & White, J. B. (2008). Why it pays to get inside the head of your opponent: The differential effects of perspective-taking and empathy in negotiations. *Psychological Science, 19*(4), 378–384.

Giridharadas, A. (2011, July 15). Real change requires politics. *New York Times*. Retrieved from https://www.nytimes.com/2011/07/16/us/16iht-currents16.html

Gomez, P.Y., & Korine, H. (2008). *Entrepreneurs and democracy: A political theory of corporate governance*. Cambridge, UK: Cambridge University Press.

Grenfell, M. (2004). *Pierre Bordieu: Agent provocateur*. London, UK: Continuum.

Holmgren, C., & From, G. (2005). Taylorism of the mind: Entrepreneurship education from a perspective of educational research. *European Educational Research Journal, 4*(4), 382–390. doi:10.2304/eerj.2005.4.4.4

Jones, S. (2014). Gendered discourses of entrepreneurship in UK higher education: The fictive entrepreneur and the fictive student. *International Small Business Journal, 32*(3), 237–258. doi:10.1177/0266242612453933

King, P. M., & Kitchner, K. S. (1994). *Developing reflective judgment*. San Francisco, CA: Jossey-Bass.

Kliewer, B. W. (2013). Why the civic engagement movement cannot achieve democratic and justice aims. *Michigan Journal of Community Service Learning, 19*(2), 72–79.

Lewin, K. (1938). *The conceptual representation and the measurement of psychological forces*. Durham, NC: Duke University Press.

Lewis, P., & Llewellyn, N. (2004). Enterprise and entrepreneurial identity. *International Journal of Entrepreneurship and Innovation, 5*(1), 5–8. doi:10.5367/000000004772913737

Light, P. (2011). *Driving social change: How to solve the world's toughest problems*. Hoboken, NJ: John Wiley & Sons.

Malone, D., Clifford, J., Anderson, A., & Serra, M. (2015, November). *The changing perceptions of millennials: Emerging views of service-learning and community engagement*. Paper presented at the meeting of the International Association for Research on Service Learning & Community Engagement, Boston, MA.

McBride, A. M., & Mlyn, E. (2016). Social innovation and civic engagement: Toward a shared future? *Diversity & Democracy, 19*(3), 4–7.

Mitchell, T. D. (2008, Spring). Traditional vs. critical service-learning: Engaging the literature to differentiate two models. *Michigan Journal of Community Service Learning*, 50–65.

Mitchell, T. D. (2010, Fall). Review essay: Challenges and possibilities: Linking social justice and service-learning. *Michigan Journal of Community Service-Learning, 17*(1), 94–97. Retrieved from https://quod.lib.umich.edu/m/mjcsl/3239521.0017.108/1

Mitchell, T. D., & Soria, K. M. (2016). Seeking social justice: Undergraduates' engagement in social change and social justice at American research universities. In K. M. Soria & T. D. Mitchell (Eds.), *Civic engagement and community service at research universities: Engaging undergraduates for social justice, social change and responsible citizenship* (pp. 241–262). London, UK: Palgrave Macmillan.

Nash, M. (2015, October). Intro to human-centered design for social impact [Workshop]. Retrieved from https://www.dropbox.com/sh/zj9532imxfajpgy/

AACdpOI9aTNgetgorrF98iqfa/2015-2016?dl=0&preview=Human+Centered+Design+Workshop+(Delivered)+Nash+10-19-15.pdf

National Service-Learning Clearinghouse. (2001). *What is service-learning?* Washington, DC: Corporation for National and Community Service.

Peredo, A. M., & Chrisman, J. J. (2006). Toward a theory of community-based enterprise. *The Academy of Management Review, 31*(2), 309–328.

Perry, W. G. (1970). *Forms of intellectual and ethical development in the college years: A scheme.* New York, NY: Holt, Rinehart and Winston.

Phills, J. A., Deiglmeier, K., & Miller, D. T. (2008). Rediscovering social innovation. *Stanford Social Innovation Review.* Retrieved from https://ssir.org/articles/entry/rediscovering_social_innovation

Piaget, J. (1967). *The child's conception of the world.* New York, NY: Routledge.

Pittaway, L., & Cope, J. (2007). Entrepreneurship education: A systematic review of the evidence. *International Small Business Journal, 25*(5), 479–510. doi:10.1177/0266242607080656

Raddon, M.-B., & Harrison, B. (2015). Is service-learning the kind face of the neoliberal university? *The Canadian Journal of Higher Education, 45*(2), 134–153.

Schnaubelt, T., & SchwartzCoffey, C. (2016). Public service and civic engagement: Multiple pathways to social change. *Diversity & Democracy, 19*(3), 24–25.

Scobey, D. (2015). *Social entrepreneurship & the business of civic engagement.* Speech presented at the Social Entrepreneurship & the Business of Civic Engagement Panel, Durham, NC. Retrieved from https://entrepreneurship.duke.edu/news-item/social-entrepreneurship-the-business-of-civic-engagement-panel/

Slaughter, S., & Rhodes, G. (2009). *Academic capitalism and the new economy: Markets, state, and higher education.* Baltimore, MD: Johns Hopkins University Press.

Soria, K. M., & Mitchell, T. D. (2016). *Civic engagement and community service at research universities: Engaging undergraduates for social justice, social change and responsible citizenship.* London, UK: Palgrave Macmillan.

Steele, C. M. (1988). The psychology of self-affirmation: Sustaining the integrity of the self. In L. Berkowitz (Ed.), *Advances in experimental social psychology* (pp. 261–302). San Diego, CA: Academic Press.

Stewart, T., & Webster, N. S. (Eds.). (2011). *Exploring cultural dynamics and tensions within service-learning.* Charlotte, NC: Information Age.

Tedmanson, D., Verduyn, K., Essers, C., & Gartner, W. B. (2012). Critical perspectives in entrepreneurship research. *Organization, 19*(5), 531–541.

Thekaekara, M. M., & Thekaekara, S. (2007). *Social justice and social entrepreneurship: Contradictory or complementary.* Oxford, UK: Skoll Centre for Social Entrepreneurship.

Thompson, R. (2013). *Changing the conversation about higher education.* Lanham, MD: Rowman & Littlefield Education.

PART THREE

THE ANCHOR INSTITUTION APPROACH

Chapter Five

CIVIC AND COMMUNITY ENGAGEMENT AND SOCIAL INNOVATION AS COMPONENTS OF A DEMOCRATIC ANCHOR INSTITUTION APPROACH

Matthew Hartley, Rita A. Hodges, Ira Harkavy, and Joann Weeks

Whereas, with regard to our anchor strategies, it is not enough to ask our faculty, staff, and students to be good citizens. The university has to be a good citizen.—James T. Harris III, president, University of San Diego (personal communication, interview with R.A. Hodges June 9, 2017)

Since the mid-1990s, there has been a growing recognition that colleges and universities have a critical role to play in the economy and the life of their cities or regions as anchor institutions (Cisneros, 1995; Harkavy

& Zuckermann, 1999; Hodges & Dubb, 2012). Higher education institutions possess enormous resources (especially human resources). They develop and transmit new knowledge; educate for careers, advancement, and citizenship; function as centers of artistic and cultural creativity; and have a significant influence on the norms, values, and practices of the pre-K–12 schooling system. In addition to their role as educators and knowledge producers, they are catalysts and hubs for local and regional economies as employers, real estate developers, clients for area vendors, and incubators for business and technology. In cities that have experienced a decrease in capital investments and the departure of industrial jobs, institutions of higher learning often serve as critical sources of employment and stability.

Seeing anchors solely in terms of their economic impact such as local procurement, real estate, and employment is a narrow and incomplete view. A comprehensive anchor approach involves the strategic alignment of the full range of resources of the university—economic, human, academic, and cultural—in a mutually beneficial and transformative partnership with the local community. In other words, the anchor institution approach focuses on how the activity of the entire institution affects the community. We have found the concept of anchor institution to be useful because it encompasses a wide range of community-based engagement activities.

Universities have deep civic roots. Although the terminology institutions have used to describe community-based work has varied over time, the idea of an anchor institution is one that the University of Pennsylvania (Penn) and a number of other institutions have found useful for describing sustained, in-depth partnership work in the community. Although there are other related terms used on Penn's campus (social innovation, academically based community service, community nursing), in our view these represent distinct approaches. *Anchor institution* offers a broader framing, one based on long-term, reciprocal partnerships where Penn is one actor among many seeking to strengthen community and democracy.

Over the last few decades, there has been a growing movement for university-community engagement that recalls the founding civic purposes of higher education (Benson et al., 2017). A number of university leaders have dedicated academic and/or institutional resources to various engagement strategies, including service-learning, volunteer projects, community-based participatory research, social innovation projects, and community economic development (Hartley, Saltmarsh, & Clayton, 2010). Such initiatives may share some similarities but often have different primary purposes, processes, and products. Importantly, if the work is not done in a thoughtful, strategic, democratic way with the goal of mutual change, then it has the potential to do more harm than good, including displacing existing residents and/or exploiting vulnerable populations. For us, a democratic approach involves a conscious and high level of transparency, as well as working "*with* the community, not *on* or *in* the community" (Benson, Harkavy, & Puckett, 2007, p. 105). Among other things, it requires the university, in Langston Hughes's (1968) wonderful phrase, "[to] listen eloquently." From our own experience, implementing such an approach also necessitates a sustained commitment, mutual learning and relearning, and very hard work.

Despite the growth of civic and community engagement over the past three decades, the actual involvement between universities and their communities has varied considerably, from neglect to episodic engagement to deep, sustained partnership. We, of course, are arguing for the development of truly engaged universities in which a very high priority is given to not only significantly improving the quality of life in the local community but also working *with* the community respectfully, collaboratively, and democratically. In addition, helping to develop and implement solutions to strategic, community-identified local problems functions as a curriculum, text, *and* performance test for a truly engaged university's research, teaching, and learning activities. No urban university (including Penn), as far as we can tell, presently meets these criteria (Harkavy, 2016). Moreover, many communities that surround urban college campuses in the United States continue to suffer from poverty, inadequate health care, and failing public schools. It is essential for universities as key anchor institutions to significantly and effectively contribute to reducing the pervasive, ongoing, seemingly intractable problems of the communities of which they are a part.

Still, Penn and other institutions have made progress in the face of significant obstacles that impede the development of truly engaged universities. Recognizing and realizing its position as an anchor institution in West Philadelphia/Philadelphia did not come readily to Penn. It has been a 30-plus-year trajectory from President Sheldon Hackney's initial acknowledgment in the 1987–1988 annual report (University of Pennsylvania, 1988) that the fates of Penn and the city were inextricably linked to President Amy Gutmann's expansive statement in the 2008–2009 financial report that "local engagement is . . . an integral part of the University's mission" (University of Pennsylvania, 2009, p. 3).

Higher Education Engagement Strategies

Academics, institutional leaders, and outside partners use different words and phrases to describe community engagement activity by colleges and universities. Two terms that have current prominence on many campuses are *civic engagement* and *social innovation*. To perhaps oversimplify, civic engagement focuses on developing students as citizens while they engage with real-world problems and working to make universities better institutional citizens. Social innovation is primarily about cultivating innovative, scalable approaches to solving social problems. We believe that these are fundamentally two different approaches, with both strengths and deficits. As McBride and Mlyn (2016) describe,

> The fundamental values of the two approaches differ. Broadly described, social innovation values disruption and being the outsider, measurement of change, and a financial bottom line, while civic engagement values collaboration and working from within, the experience of change, and secondary financial success. (p. 5)

We believe that these differences emerge in part based on their origins, with civic engagement rooted in student and academic affairs, and social innovation having emerged primarily from the business world. Although we recognize that the work is evolving, it is important to consider these roots.

Sandra Enos (2015) notes the commonalities and distinctions between service-learning and social entrepreneurship (which we consider the dominant forms of civic engagement and social innovation, respectively). Key commonalities include a focus on helping to solve social problems, often in the areas of education, health, poverty, and community development; partnerships with communities; and efforts to change higher education. McBride and Mlyn (2016) point to the shared value between practitioners of civic engagement and social innovation as "provid[ing] opportunities for students to 'make a difference'" (p. 5).

Enos (2015) notes that the critical differences include service-learning's focus on collaboration versus social entrepreneurship's tendency toward individualistic efforts, roots in the nonprofit sector versus the business world, support of existing organizations versus founding of new ones, and educating students for citizenship and democracy versus solving problems independently of political involvement or policy change.

Neither form of engagement, of course, is without its weaknesses. McBride and Mlyn (2016) critique civic engagement for the "potential focus on charity rather than change and a tendency toward small-scale (sometimes minimally effective) interventions" (p. 5) and critique social innovation for "its potential lack of depth, respect, and follow-through" (p. 5). We explore each of these in turn.

On many campuses the predominant form of civic engagement is service-learning—purposefully linking community-based work with the curriculum. However, rarely is service-learning pervasive across the curriculum. Even when it is, it can tend to position the faculty and students as experts in the community solving problems for the community—that is, a technocratic approach. Incorporating civic engagement into the core work of the academy—making it a central aspect of teaching and learning and of research—remains a challenge (Colby, Ehrlich, Beaumont, & Stephens, 2003). There is certainly value in having students work in their local communities: It enables them to witness what is occurring there and tends to foster in participants a sense of responsibility to those communities (Astin & Sax, 1998). However, systematic instructional efforts to help students understand the complex factors that perpetuate the status quo are often missing (Saltmarsh & Hartley, 2011), as is "a well-designed service-learning program to engender participatory or activist commitments integral to a strong civic identity" (Johanek & Puckett, 2005, p. 149). Enos (2015) points out that much of service-learning today has been oriented away from social justice values and tends to be more narrowly focused on sloving discrete problems rather than working with the community as a partner for long-term change.

Social innovation has its roots in the business world and business schools. Enos (2015) offers several critiques of social entrepreneurship, which we would extend to social innovation. We find one critique particularly salient: "A broader and deeper awareness of the social context and environments within which change is proposed takes a back stage to showing the change agent as a heroic individual" (p. 63). In other words, social innovation positions the university as expert and the community as client. That duality is highly problematic. It overlooks the expertise and funds of knowledge in the community that are necessary for solving highly complex real-world problems as they are manifested locally. Moreover, social entrepreneurship tends to focus on scaling up rather than seeking effective solutions that take local culture and context into account (Enos, 2015). Partly because of these shortfalls, Ashoka U, which supports colleges and universities across the world to implement changemaker education, has sought to shift both its practice and the field from social entrepreneurship to a broader focus on social innovation, which is intended to be more inclusive and participatory (Seligsohn & Kim, 2017). As discussed by Kim and Krampetz (2016), Ashoka U draws on the definition of *social innovation* presented in the *Stanford Social Innovation Review*: "a novel solution to a social problem that is more effective, efficient, sustainable, or just than existing solutions and for which the value created accrues primarily to society as a whole rather than private individuals" (Phills, Deiglmeier, & Miller, 2008, p. 36).

McBride and Mlyn (2016) argue persuasively that a merging of the distinct strengths of these approaches—the creativity and focus of social innovation and the attention to community well-being and sustainability of civic engagement—can help move higher education toward genuine community-based solutions to our most important and pressing problems.

Some of the most promising initiatives today are built on ongoing partnerships between colleges and universities and their local communities. These partnerships involve the development of significant, serious, sustained efforts that draw together faculty, students, and community members to address community-identified real-world problems. They provide rich opportunities for students to develop the skills they need to be effective democratic-minded citizens. They give rise to research activities that link the expertise within the university with the expertise outside its walls—that is, the expertise embodied in community members who understand the local context in which problems are situated. Sustained partnerships of this kind not only foster the civic development of students but also strengthen democracy at the local level. It is worth noting that on these campuses (some of which are cited in the following sections), a serious commitment to such partnerships has led to changes in the colleges and universities themselves—altering assumptions about how we should teach and whose knowledge counts and encouraging new and broader understandings about what faculty work is important and what kind of research matters. A powerful commitment to the democratic ideal moves institutions from a commitment to promoting civic education among its students to a commitment to advancing democratic civic engagement by means of university-community partnerships (Benson et al., 2017).

Over the past several decades, enlightened self-interest has prompted many colleges and universities to respond at an institutional level to external pressures from government, foundations, and public opinion by partnering in local community economic development efforts to ameliorate such significant problems as poverty, crime, violence, and physical deterioration. Such activities also manifest a renewed historical commitment to the civic and democratic purposes of higher education. For example, the concept of anchor institutions, according to Taylor and Luter's 2013 literature review, "emerged [after 2000] as a new paradigm for understanding the role that place-based institutions could play in building successful communities and local economies" (p. 3).

Partnerships between anchor institutions and communities have gained increased impetus from the Anchor Institutions Task Force

(AITF). In 2009 the Task Force on Anchor Institutions, an ad hoc national panel, advised the U.S. Department of Housing and Urban Development on how the agency could strategically "engage urban anchor institutions, particularly institutions of higher education and academic medical centers ('Eds and Meds'), in collaborative partnerships" (Harkavy et al., 2009, p. 147) to help revitalize their local communities and regions. The task force submitted its report, *Anchor Institutions as Partners in Building Successful Communities and Local Economies* (Harkavy et al., 2009), and became a permanent, formal organization (AITF), with the mission of forging democratic civic partnerships involving anchor institutions. The AITF is guided by the core values of collaboration and partnership, equity and social justice, democracy and democratic practice, and commitment to place and community (Taylor & Luter, 2013). David Maurrasse, president of Marga Inc., is director of the AITF, a growing network of approximately 1,000 members, with Ira Harkavy continuing to serve as chair. Significantly, the development of this group as a permanent organization has helped bring the idea of anchor institutions increasingly into national academic and policy discussions.

The anchor institution concept has two distinct features, at least as we and the members of the AITF conceive it: a focus on locality and a set of values that emphasize democracy and mutual transformation. Whereas civic engagement and social innovation can be focused locally, nationally, or globally, the anchor institution concept is distinctly local. The benefits of a local community focus for college and university civic engagement programs are manifold. Ongoing, continuous interaction is facilitated through work in an easily accessible location. Relationships of trust, so essential for effective partnerships and effective learning, are also built through day-to-day work on problems and issues of mutual concern. In addition, the local community provides a convenient setting in which service-learning courses, community-based research courses, and related courses in different disciplines can work together on a complex problem to produce substantive results. Because work in a university's local community facilitates interaction across schools and disciplines, it can also create interdisciplinary learning opportunities. Finally, the local community is a democratic real-world learning site in which community members and academics can pragmatically determine whether the work is making a real difference and whether both the neighborhood and the institution are better as a result of common efforts (Benson et al., 2017).

"Anchoring is more than being present," states David Maurrasse (2013, p. 2), founding president of Marga Inc. and director of the AITF. "It is an active commitment to reducing disparities and engaging in mutually beneficial, democratic collaboration" (p. 2). As noted, the AITF was founded on the core values of collaboration and partnership, equity and social justice, democracy and democratic practice, and commitment to place and community. Maurrasse (2013) emphasizes that the task force "is uniquely functioning as a values-based movement organization" (p. 3). This stands in contrast to the "value neutral" (Hartley, 2011, p. 42) approach that has remained the dominant form of civic engagement. We believe that the anchor approach provides a set of unifying values across different forms of engagement. As long as basic democratic values are upheld, which we describe next, different strategies can bring distinct value to the community and the university.

Democratic Purpose, Process, and Product

What ultimately matters, in our view, is taking on community-based work in a democratic way and seeking democratic ends. We believe that genuine collaboration inside and outside the academy is necessary for producing innovative knowledge that solves real-world problems, preparing students to be creative and caring citizens, and creating positive changes in the human condition and in the university itself.

We strongly believe in the principles of democratic purpose, process, and product, which were identified first by higher education leaders (including Harkavy) at a 2004 conference sponsored by the Kellogg Forum on Higher Education for the Public Good as crucial for successful university-community partnerships (Boyte & Hollander, 1999). We believe operationalizing these values is particularly crucial for effective anchor-community engagement. These principles are succinctly defined as follows:

- *Purpose*: An abiding democratic and civic purpose is the rightly placed goal if higher education is to truly contribute to the public good. In our estimation, higher education's core purposes are education for democratic citizenship and the creation of knowledge to advance the human condition, which significantly involves developing and maintaining a democratic society. We argue for a participatory democracy, not just democracy in terms of voting or relative to a system of government. We see democracy as the pragmatic philosopher John Dewey (1939) saw it: as "a way of life" (p. 229), in which all citizens actively participate in all of the communal, societal, educational, and institutional decisions that significantly shape their lives (Benson et al., 2007).

- *Process*: In a democratic process, the higher education institution and the community, as well as members of both communities, treat each other as ends in themselves rather than as means to an end. The relationship itself and welfare of the various partners are the preeminent value, not developing a specified program or completing a research project. We also see democratic processes as involving inclusivity, transparency, and openness. These are the types of collaborations that tend to be significant, serious, and sustained; lead to a relationship of genuine respect and trust; and most benefit the partners and society.
- *Product*: A successful partnership also strives to make a positive difference for all partners—this is the democratic product. Contributing to the well-being of people in the community (both now and in the future) through structural community improvement should be a central goal of a truly democratic partnership for the public good. Research, teaching, and service should also be strengthened as a result of a successful partnership. Indeed, working with the community to improve the quality of life in the community may be one of the best ways to improve the quality of life and learning within a higher education institution (Harkavy & Hartley, 2009).

Democratic purpose, process, and product also necessitate engagement and innovation from both the academy and community. Nancy Cantor, Peter Englot, and Marilyn Higgins (2013) describe the importance of "[moving] beyond the one-way flow of intellectual capital (and technology transfer) independently generated within the ivory tower and given to (or perhaps foisted upon) communities" (p. 20). Instead, they argue, broad and diverse "communities of experts" should be created that include those "from within and outside the academy that draw on diverse collective expertise to make a difference" (p. 20). In other words, effective partnerships are predicated on the assumption that each partner has expertise that is important. Faculty members have disciplinary-based knowledge and community members have an understanding of the context and the environment, an understanding that is essential for actually solving real-world problems. It is, in our view, impossible to engage in meaningful work that produces results without employing a decision-making process that is based on mutuality, reciprocity, trust, and democratic principles (Cantor et al., 2013).

Moreover, Scott Page's (2017) research on the power of diversity suggests that broad and diverse communities of experts produce the best conditions for truly innovative problem-solving. Innovation, we believe, should not be about just creating new things or ideas; systemic change is needed *within* our institutions as well. This is a key part of the mutually transformative democratic product that can result from genuine, comprehensive engagement. Meaningful innovation requires institutional change; otherwise, the work will tend to be episodic, with relatively insignificant changes that present a mere illusion of progress. Put simply, innovation needs to be part of systemic change, and systemic change makes innovation sustainable.

A place-based focus particularly lends itself to involving voices from the community, whether taking a civic engagement or social innovation approach. As discussed, an inclusive epistemology that involves the knowledge possessed "on the ground" by community members is required for the effective solution of locally manifested universal problems. This epistemology expands the definition of *expertise* and knowing to include other voices—those not necessarily steeped in professional credentials or academic knowledge but in lived experience of the conditions and actualities under examination. Community members with that knowledge must also be actively involved when the problem is defined and remain involved through the development and implementation of solutions (Whyte, Greenwood, & Lazes, 1989).

Moving Beyond Current Challenges

Different conceptions of engagement approaches, as well as tendencies to work in silos, have created tension on individual campuses and in the field. As a report published in 1982 by the Organisation for Economic Co-operation and Development titled *The University and the Community* aptly put it, "Communities have problems, universities have departments" (Center for Educational Research and Innovation, 1982, p. 127). Quite simply, the unintegrated, fragmented, internally conflictual structure and organization of colleges and universities impede the development of solutions to highly complex human and societal problems. Changing this requires colleges and universities to address the division between and among the arts and sciences and the professions and to actively construct efforts that bring together different funds of knowledge (including those in the community) to address real-world problems. Compounding this situation is what might be called the disciplinary fallacy afflicting American universities—namely, the misconception that faculty members are duty bound to serve only the scholastic interests and preoccupations of their disciplines and have neither the responsibility nor the capacity to help their universities keep their long-standing promise to prepare undergraduates for lives of moral and civic responsibility (Fish, 2008).

Our efforts to address fragmentation and increase collaborative alignment have been significantly informed by Muzafer Sherif's (1958) superordinate goal theory. He defined *superordinate goals* as

> goals which are compelling and highly appealing to members of two or more groups in conflict which cannot be attained by the resources and energies of the groups separately. In effect, they are goals attained only when groups pull together. (pp. 349–350)

Identifying significant, complex local problems that people care deeply about is a way to draw together expertise from inside and outside the university; it can also help align the work of various departments, centers, institutes, and schools within the university. In practice, the long-standing competitive fragmentation built into the organizational culture and structure of higher education institutions has often trumped the logic of collaboration and enlightened self-interest. As a result, until recently, attempts to apply Sherif's superordinate goal theory have produced only limited success.

In the next section, we turn to the case we know best: Penn's work as an anchor institution in West Philadelphia, its local geographic community. By continuing to focus its resources and efforts on complex problems that are both widely recognized as very important and require the effective integration of specialized knowledge and skills, Penn can successfully apply superordinate goal theory, simultaneously reducing its competitive fragmentation and increasing its interdisciplinary, interschool collaboration.

Toward an Integrated Democratic Anchor Institution–Community Partnerships Approach

Penn's evolving, unified approach as an anchor institution involves the engagement of both the academic and institutional sides of the university, led by the Netter Center for Community Partnerships and the Office of the Executive President, respectively.

Since the mid-1980s, Penn has developed academically based community service courses, coordinated by the Netter Center, in which service is rooted in and intrinsically tied to research, teaching, and learning, and in which the goal of the courses is to contribute to structural community improvement. In 2018–2019, across 9 of Penn's 12 schools, 74 Academically Based Community Service (ABCS) courses were taught, engaging approximately 1,700 Penn students (undergraduate, graduate, and professional). Over the past few decades, an increasing number of faculty members from a wide range of Penn schools and departments have revised existing courses or created new courses, providing innovative curricular opportunities for their students to become active learners, creative real-world problem-solvers, and active producers (as opposed to passive consumers) of knowledge.

For example, in 1991 Professor Francis Johnston, a renowned expert on nutritional anthropology concluded a lengthy term as chair of the anthropology department and decided to redesign a course, Anthropology 210, to focus on helping to solve the community-identified problem of poor nutrition. Johnston began work with the community through an approach that embodied democratic purpose, process, and product from its inception. The work began at Turner Middle School, where the teachers had recognized that the standard snack of potato chips and colored sugar water was not contributing to their students' health or academic success. A democratic purpose—improving the health and nutrition of schoolchildren—had been identified, leading to Johnston's redesigned course, Anthropology 310: Nutrition, Health, and Community Schools, which became the prototype for ABCS courses.

The initial class of 18 Penn students worked with Turner sixth-grade students on a range of small-scale participatory action research projects dealing with healthy foods, physical growth, dietary intake, and obesity status. The results were used in planning subsequent activities with school youth, teachers, and Penn students and faculty, adhering to a democratic process that engaged all stakeholders. Anthropology 310's success not only influenced the anthropology department (which went on to develop an academic track in public interest anthropology) but also inspired other Penn departments and schools to become involved. Over the next few years, a widening circle of Penn faculty and students worked with Johnston in collaboration with local middle school teachers and students to understand the nutritional practices in the community and to address the problem through a series of jointly developed projects. These included an educational program, an in-school market that provided healthy snacks, a school-based garden, and a nutritional outreach program for the community. Ultimately, Johnston's course led to the development of the Agatston Urban Nutrition Initiative (AUNI), a central Netter Center program that engages approximately 6,000 students and their families across 16 Philadelphia public schools, as well as hundreds of adult community members at a variety of West Philadelphia community and senior centers. This ongoing mutually beneficial partnership among Penn, the local schools, and now the wider community is the sustainable democratic product of Johnston's initial engagement at Turner Middle School.

One particular innovation that grew out of an AUNI school day nutrition project is Rebel Ventures (RV). In 2010, 10 eighth-grade students came up with the idea for a project to create and sell a healthy snack to their peers. A small group of Penn students engaged in ABCS courses was brought on board to help start this classroom-based business, and a granola bar business was born. RV quickly developed into an after-school job-training program, and from 2012 to 2016, the youth made handmade and hand-packed granola bars (Rebel Bars) in a rented commercial kitchen space and distributed them locally to schools and stores. In 2015, RV formed a not-for-profit, youth-run social enterprise supported by the Netter Center. RV continues to engage high school, undergraduate, and graduate students in all aspects of a business enterprise through social entrepreneurship, including researching and developing healthy recipes, as well as marketing, accounting, and distributing products based on those recipes. Their latest product is Rebel Crumbles, a fruit-filled, whole-grain breakfast cake that is distributed throughout the School District of Philadelphia and Archdiocesan schools, with more than 1.3 million Crumbles served to Philadelphia schoolchildren since 2017. It is the first youth-created food item served in a school meals program in any major city. A relationship with a local distributor also helps bring Crumbles to other retail locations, including local supermarkets and catering vendors on Penn's campus.

AUNI and RV are part of the Netter Center's University-Assisted Community Schools (UACS) program. UACS educates, engages, empowers, and serves not only students but also all other members of the community, providing an organizing framework for bringing Netter Center programs, including ABCS courses, to West Philadelphia schools. UACS focuses on schools as core institutions for community engagement and democratic development, as well as connects school day and after-school curricula to solve locally identified, real-world, community problems (Harkavy & Hartley, 2009). Currently the Netter Center supports comprehensive programming at seven primary UACS sites, of which four are K–8 and three are high schools. It also has partnership activities at several additional schools. The Netter Center conceptualizes ABCS and UACS as part of Penn's larger anchor institution approach.

Not to minimize the accomplishments described, but academic engagement alone is insufficient to make the needed changes. The involvement of the entire university is called for if genuine progress is to be made. By *beginning* to consciously integrate its academic and its institutional efforts for community improvement, Penn is mobilizing increased resources to better realize its mission as an engaged anchor institution.

The Netter Center works in close partnership with the Office of the Executive Vice President, for example, on issues of community economic development that help advance Penn's role as an anchor. Penn's Economic Inclusion Program engages local, minority, and women-owned businesses and residents in the university's economic activity. Penn launched its "Buy West Philadelphia" program in the 1980s, for example, to direct its purchasing dollars to local vendors, and the program has continued to grow since then. In fiscal year 2015, Penn spent $122 million with businesses in West Philadelphia, approximately 13% of total purchasing of goods and services (University of Pennsylvania, 2015). Penn partners with city entities, such as the Minority Business Enterprise Center, to help build capacity for small, local suppliers. For all campus construction projects of $5 million or more, Penn has committed to awarding 25% of contracts to minority- and women-owned companies and to having 20% of the workforce consist of minorities and women. In fiscal year 2015, Penn and the University of Pennsylvania Health System hired 1,572 local residents (47.5% of all new hires). In housing development, since 1998, Penn's Enhanced Mortgage Program has provided more than 1,000 grants to staff and faculty as an incentive to choose West Philadelphia to live in. Penn also created a Neighborhood Preservation and Development Fund in the mid-1990s to secure several hundred units of apartments at below market price, to ensure equity among housing, while also creating new market rate housing (University of Pennsylvania, n.d.).

Penn helped create a special services district, University City District (UCD), in 1997 to clean the streets and help patrol alongside Penn's own new police force and city police. Today, UCD is a 26-member board representing "eds and meds," local businesses and nonprofits, and residents, chaired by Penn's executive vice president, Craig Carnaroli, with a much broader vision. Between 2011 and 2017, UCD trained approximately 785 local residents for jobs at Penn and other local anchor institutions through its West Philadelphia Skills Initiative, with more than 90% of recent graduates connected to employment (University City District, 2019).

Amy Gutmann, Penn's current president, a distinguished political philosopher whose scholarly work explores the role public schools and universities play in advancing democracy and democratic societies, has taken the university's engagement to the next level. In her 2004 presidential inaugural address, Gutmann unveiled the "Penn Compact," a statement of "our boldest aspirations for higher education," (para. 33) which she enumerated as follows: "to increase access, to integrate knowledge, and to engage locally and globally" (para. 65). Significantly, the compact recognizes local engagement as a way for Penn to achieve eminence as a research university. Gutmann is the university's first president to create an institutional advancement strategy linked to local engagement.

Not all engagement efforts have a primary focus on Penn and West Philadelphia, of course. Within the Wharton School of Business, for example, the Wharton Social Impact Initiative works to advance the research and practice of social impact, including through experiential learning and fellowship opportunities for students from West Philadelphia to sub-Saharan Africa.

Although these and other academic and institutional efforts are indicators of genuine progress, Penn still has a very long way to go to comprehensively and effectively engage and align its various components and substantial resources in democratic, sustained, mutually transformative partnerships with its community.

Other Promising Institutional Examples

In the constellation of American higher education institutions, Penn is a relatively large and very well-resourced research university. Colleagues from other institutions have, from time to time, raised important questions about whether institutions that are not as large or are less well resourced can reasonably take on the work of an anchor. In fact, a number of colleges and universities, ones that represent the diversity of our system of higher education, have also found the anchor institution concept to be a useful one for describing their deep, sustained, and democratic partnership work in their community. We briefly touch on examples from two other institutions, Rutgers University–Newark (RU-N), a public research university, and the University of San Diego (USD), a private Catholic institution, both of which have developed strategic plans focused on an anchor institution agenda. A clear mission and strategic plan help institutions present consistent priorities, which, in turn, contribute to programmatic cohesion among the various areas of the college or university (Hartley, 2002).

RU-N developed a strategic plan in 2014 with the following eight priorities:

1. Invest in collaboration in academic and research programs
2. Invest in our students
3. Invest in our faculty and graduate and professional students
4. Value our professional and support staff as key to our success
5. Invest in the spaces and places where we live, learn, create, and engage the world
6. Invest in anchor institution collaboration
7. Leverage our diversity and building civic dialogue
8. Tell the [RU-N] story more effectively ([RU-N], 2017, p. 1)

RU-N's anchor agenda involves the integration of academic and economic resources to address five major areas in Newark: building strong educational pathways (pre-K through 16) for increased postsecondary attainment; developing strong, healthy, and safe neighborhoods; promoting and leveraging the arts and culture; incorporating science in the urban environment; and encouraging equitable growth through entrepreneurship and economic development. The following are examples of work now in process are (a) the Newark City of Learning Collaborative, a coalition of more than 40 cross-sector partners supported by the university that aims to raise the college attainment rate in Newark from 17% to 25% by 2025 and (b) the Newark Public Safety Collaborative, a public-private-nonprofit working group convened by the office of the mayor, RU-N, and local corporate and philanthropic leaders that is implementing an evidence-based, city-wide public safety strategy. Chancellor Nancy Cantor sees the anchor institution approach as part of her university's identity and operational strategy (N. Cantor, personal communication, June 9, 2017), and leaders across sectors in Newark are starting to use the phrase *anchor institution* (P. Englot, personal communication, June 12, 2017).

USD's strategic plan, Envisioning 2024, identifies 6 interconnected pathways to achieve its vision, or what President James Harris describes as "set[ting] a standard for contemporary Catholic universities through innovative changemaking to address humanity's greatest challenges" (University of San Diego, 2016). The 6 pathways are anchor institution, engaged scholarship, practice of changemaking, access and inclusion, care for our common home, and liberal arts education for the twenty-first century (University of San Diego, 2016). USD is also 1 of approximately 40 institutions designated by Ashoka U as a changemaker campus, which recognizes global leaders in social innovation and changemaking in higher education. And USD is 1 of only 10 campuses recognized by both Ashoka

U and Carnegie Community Engagement Classification (Enos, 2015). While Ashoka U helps define "individuals' roles as changemakers," says Harris, "the anchor strategy defines the institution's role" in changemaking (J. Harris, personal communication, June 9, 2017).

"To be a great international university we must first be an anchor institution for our local community," also states Harris (University of San Diego, 2016, para. 3). USD is particularly invested in the immediate neighborhood of Linda Vista, in which many of the local residents are distressed (as described in chapter six of this volume). In fall 2013, the university's Changemaker Hub and Mulvaney Center for Community, Awareness and Social Action launched the Impact Linda Vista Initiative to strengthen the community and engage university students and local residents in the codevelopment of innovative social initiatives in this community. The anchor institution pathway of the new strategic plan demonstrates a commitment of the institution to local engagement at the highest level. It also provides an opportunity to coordinate various stakeholders and community engagement activities around a common anchor agenda (D. Maurrasse, personal communication, September 12, 2017).

A particularly urgent area that the university is focused deeply on is homelessness—a universal problem that it is helping to solve locally. As a key anchor institution in the area, USD is convening other anchors, local government officials, business and nonprofit leaders, and funders to discuss innovative solutions to the problem of homelessness. The university has hosted more than 20 symposiums on homelessness over the past 2 years alone (J. Harris, personal communication, October 21, 2019). USD has also developed an anchor board comprising university and community stakeholders to help guide its overall strategy as an anchor institution (C. Nayve, personal communication, June 12, 2017).

Conclusion

We have found the anchor institution concept particularly powerful, as have some of our colleagues, because of its attention to democratic purpose, process, and product, as well as its focus on locality. The anchor concept and its democratic values also have the power to unify the concepts of social innovation and civic engagement. In our judgment, what matters most is a clear commitment to a set of values. For us, this is strengthening democracy and communities and doing so in a way that is mutually beneficial and transformational for both the university and its neighbors. The strategy that we have found to be the most promising is the identification of *superordinate goals*—critically important major problems that members inside and outside the university feel are of vital importance and that require the expertise and energies of all involved if progress is to be made toward their solution. The term one uses to describe these activities or the specific approach matters little as long as the focus remains on democratic purpose, process, and product. If these democratic values are upheld, then meaningful gains can be realized.

In this chapter, we have tried to provide some comparison between different conceptions of community engagement work, arguing for the anchor institution concept as the unifying strategy to advance teaching and research at universities and improve the quality of life in our local communities. We have provided a brief overview of institutional efforts to support Penn's role as an anchor institution, dedicated to creating sustainable, democratic partnerships with its neighbors in West Philadelphia. This civic imperative has been an aspirational ideal since Penn's founding by Benjamin Franklin. Increased faculty and student involvement through academically based community service; the development of numerous sustained, democratic partnerships in the community; and the growing investment of institutional resources to support community economic development make it clear that we have come a long, long way. But we have miles and miles to go. We have also shared brief examples from our colleagues in Newark and San Diego.

To conclude by placing our argument in a larger context, we again turn to the work of the great American philosopher and educator John Dewey, who famously wrote, "Democracy must begin at home, and its home is the neighborly community" (Dewey, 1927/1954, p. 213). In effect, we are updating Dewey and advocating the following proposition: *Democracy must begin at home, and its home is the truly engaged neighborly university and its local community partners.* Neighborliness, we contend, is the primary indicator that an institution is working for the public good.

For Dewey (1910), knowledge and learning are most effectively advanced when human beings work collaboratively to solve specific, important real-world problems in "a *forked-road* situation, a situation which is ambiguous, which presents a dilemma, which poses alternatives" (p. 11, italics in original). Focusing on universal problems—for example, poverty, poor schooling, and inadequate health care—that are manifested locally is, in our judgment, the best way to apply Dewey's brilliant proposition. A focus on local engagement through the anchor institution concept, we contend, is an extraordinarily promising strategy for realizing institutional mission and purpose.

In short, we are advocating for every university to be truly engaged—that is, comprehensive, democratic, significant, serious, and sustained involvement of *all* aspects of the university (including integration of academic and institutional resources)—with its local community. Approaches of civic engagement and social innovation, which may well conflict, can be part of a strategy for realizing the superordinate goal of creating and sustaining just, democratic universities, communities, and societies. To make genuine progress toward reaching that goal, we believe, requires the full commitment of the university to become a truly engaged, democratic anchor institution.

References

Astin, A. W., & Sax L. (1998). How undergraduates are affected by service participation. *Journal of College Student Development, 39*, 251–263.

Benson, L., Harkavy, I., & Puckett, J. (2007). *Dewey's dream: Universities and democracies in an age of education reform.* Philadelphia, PA: Temple University Press.

Benson, L., Harkavy, I., Puckett, J., Hartley, M., Hodges, R. A., Johnston, F. E., & Weeks, J. (2017). *Knowledge for social change: Bacon, Dewey, and the revolutionary transformation of research universities in the twenty-first century.* Philadelphia, PA: Temple University Press.

Boyte, H., & Hollander, E. (1999). *Wingspread declaration on renewing the civic mission of the American research university.* Report prepared on behalf of the participants at the December 1998 and July 1999 Wingspread conferences. Boston, MA: Campus Compact. Retrieved from https://files.eric.ed.gov/fulltext/ED435370.pdf

Cantor, N., Englot, P., & Higgins, M. (2013). Making the work of anchor institutions stick: Building coalitions and collective expertise. *Journal of Higher Education Outreach & Engagement, 17*(3), 20–21. Retrieved from http://openjournals.libs.uga.edu/index.php/jheoe/article/view/1036

Center for Educational Research and Innovation. (1982). *The university and the community: The problems of changing relationships.* Paris, France: Organisation for Economic Co-operation and Development.

Cisneros, H. G. (1995). *The university and the urban challenge.* Washington, DC: U.S. Department of Housing and Urban Development.

Colby, A., Ehrlich T., Beaumont E., & Stephens J. (2003). *Educating citizens: Preparing America's undergraduates for lives of moral and civic responsibility.* San Francisco, CA: Jossey-Bass.

Dewey, J. (1910). *How we think.* Boston, MA: D.C. Heath.

Dewey, J. (1939). Creative democracy—the task before us. In D. Morris & I. Shapiro (Eds.), *John Dewey: The political writings* (pp. 240–245). Indianapolis, IN: Hackett.

Dewey J. (1954). *The public and its problems.* Denver, CO: Swallow Press/Ohio University Press. (Original work published 1927)

Enos, S. L. (2015). *Service-learning and social entrepreneurship in higher education: A pedagogy of social change.* London, UK: Palgrave Macmillan.

Fish, S. (2008). *Save the world on your own time.* New York, NY: Oxford University Press.

Gutmann, A. (2004, October 15). Inaugural address. Retrieved from http://www.upenn.edu/secretary/inauguration/speech.html

Harkavy, I. (2016). Engaging urban universities as anchor institutions for health equity. *American Journal of Public Health, 106*(12), 2155–2157.

Harkavy, I., Birch, E., Alperovitz, G., Cantor, N., Clancy, G., Coletta, C., . . . Weeks, J. (2009). Anchor institutions as partners in building successful communities and local economies. In P. C. Brophy & R. D. Godsil (Eds.), *Retooling HUD for a catalytic federal government: A report to Secretary Shaun Donovan* (pp. 147–169). Philadelphia, PA: Penn Institute for Urban Research, University of Pennsylvania.

Harkavy, I., & Hartley, M. (2009, Summer). University-school-community partnerships for youth development and democratic renewal. *New Directions in Youth Development,* 122, 7–18.

Harkavy, I., & Zuckerman, H. (1999, August). *Eds and meds: Cities' hidden assets.* The Brookings Institution Survey Series. Washington, DC: Center on Urban & Metropolitan Policy, The Brookings Institution.

Hartley, M. (2002). *A call to purpose: Mission-centered change at three liberal arts colleges.* New York, NY: RoutledgeFalmer.

Hartley, M. (2011). Idealism and compromise and the civic engagement movement. In J. Saltmarsh & M. Hartley (Eds.), *"To serve a larger purpose": Engagement for democracy and the transformation of higher education* (pp. 27–48). Philadelphia, PA: Temple University Press.

Hartley, M., Saltmarsh, J., & Clayton, P. (2010). Is the civic engagement movement changing higher education? *British Journal of Educational Studies,* 58, 391–406.

Hodges, R. A., & Dubb, S. (2012). *The road half traveled: University engagement at a crossroads.* East Lansing: Michigan State University Press.

Hughes, L. (1968). *The best of simple.* New York: Hill and Wang.

Johanek, M. C., & Puckett, J. (2005). The state of civic education: Preparing citizens in an era of accountability. In S. Fuhrman & M. Lazerson (Eds.), *Institutions of American democracy: The public schools* (pp. 130–159). Oxford, UK: Oxford University Press.

Kim, M., & Krampetz, E. (2016). The rise of the sophisticated changemaker. *Diversity & Democracy, 19*(3). Retrieved from https://www.aacu.org/diversity-democracy/2016/summer/kim

Maurrasse, D. (2013). From the desk of the guest editor. *Journal of Higher Education Outreach and Engagement, 17*(3), 1–6.

McBride, A. M., & Mlyn, E. (2016). Social innovation and civic engagement: Toward a shared future? *Diversity & Democracy, 19*(3), 4–7.

Page, S. (2017). *The diversity bonus: How great teams pay off in the knowledge economy.* Princeton, NJ: Princeton University Press.

Phills, J. A., Jr., Deiglmeier, K., & Miller, D. T. (2008, Fall). Rediscovering social innovation. *Stanford Social Innovation Review.* Retrieved from https://ssir.org/articles/entry/rediscovering_social_innovation

Rutgers University–Newark. (2017). *Rutgers University–Newark: Where opportunity meets excellence spring 2017 update.* Retrieved from http://www.newark. rutgers.edu/sites/default/files/ru-n_strategic_plan_update_spring_2017_w-appendices.pdf

Saltmarsh, J. A., & Hartley, M. (2011). Democratic engagement. In J. A. Saltmarsh & M. Hartley (Eds.), *To serve a larger purpose* (pp. 14–26). Philadelphia, PA: Temple University Press.

Seligsohn, A., & Kim, M. (2017). Compact Nation Podcast: Season 1 Episode 10. Retrieved from https://compact.org/podcast/season1-episode10/

Sherif, M. (1958). Superordinate goals in the reduction of intergroup conflict. *American Journal of Sociology, 63*, 349–356.

Taylor, H., & Luter, G. (2013). *Anchor institutions: An interpretative review essay.* New York, NY: Anchor Institutions Task Force.

University City District. (2019). West Philadelphia Skills Initiative: Results and impact. Retrieved from https://www.universitycity.org/wpsi/

University of Pennsylvania. (1988). *University of Pennsylvania Annual Report 1987–88: Penn and Philadelphia: Common ground.* Philadelphia: Office of Publications Marketing Communications, University Relations, University of Pennsylvania.

University of Pennsylvania. (2009). *University of Pennsylvania Financial Report 2008–2009: Engaging locally.* Philadelphia: Office of the Vice President for Finance and Treasurer, University of Pennsylvania.

University of Pennsylvania. (2015). *Impact: University of Pennsylvania powering Philadelphia and Pennsylvania.* Philadelphia: Office of the Executive Vice President, University of Pennsylvania. Retrieved from http://www.evp.upenn.edu/pdf/Penn_Economic_Impact_Powering_PHL_PA.pdf

University of Pennsylvania. (n.d.). *Community and economic development.* Philadelphia: Office of the Executive Vice President, University of Pennsylvania. Retrieved from http://www.evp.upenn.edu/strategic-initiatives/community-and-economic-development.html

University of San Diego. (2016). Envisioning 2024. Retrieved from https://www.sandiego.edu/envisioning-2024/overview/

Whyte, W. F., Greenwood, D. J., & Lazes, P. (1989). Participatory action research: Through practice to science. *American Behavioral Scientist, 32*(5), 513–551.

Chapter Six

COMMUNITY ENGAGEMENT, SOCIAL INNOVATION, AND ANCHOR INSTITUTIONS

A Case Study for Converging Paradigms of Social Justice Education

Kevin Guerrieri, Sandra Sgoutas-Emch, Chris Nayve, Judith Liu, Juan Carlos Rivas, and Mike Williams

The University of San Diego (USD) has historically been dedicated to public service and the development of civically engaged individuals. Since its founding in 1949, USD has embraced socially responsible action that improves the human condition, promotes deep reflection and empathy, and cultivates an ecosystem that generates knowledge for the good of society, all of which reflect the institution's focus on the liberal arts education, its commitment to social justice, and its faith-based identity in relation to the Catholic intellectual tradition. Its mission statement identifies USD as "a Roman Catholic institution committed to advancing academic excellence, expanding liberal and professional knowledge, creating a diverse and inclusive community, and preparing leaders dedicated to ethical conduct and compassionate service" (University of San Diego, n.d.).

Having a mission and core values that align with Catholic social teaching has been important at the university historically for laying the foundation on which to build programming in conjunction with community partnerships and to foster civic engagement opportunities. Parting from this initial faith-based foundation, USD has integrated several developments through the years that reflect the institution's commitment to the public good and also align with broader, national tendencies; these include the expansion of community engagement, the incorporation of social innovation, and the articulation of an anchor institution discourse. The evolution of these developments has doubtlessly contributed to the overall work of social justice in the San Diego community and beyond. However, the diverging approaches and practices have also produced gaps and tensions, and a need remains for more profound assessment of actual impact on the community, in both quantitative and qualitative terms. In this chapter, we trace this institutional narrative as a case study, identifying both challenges and opportunities at each historical period as the different approaches and practices emerged. Then we provide a set of five guidelines, which are informed by the case study, and conclude by presenting ongoing challenges and new directions.

From Missionary Work and Charity to Community Engagement

The Catholic Church's social teaching is focused on "building a just society and living lives of holiness amidst the challenges of modern society" (United States Conference of Catholic Bishops, n.d.). The seven tenets of Catholic social teaching require direct engagement with one's community through a variety of modalities (Kaczor, 2007). Historically, for the church, these modalities have primarily included missionary immersions and acts of charity. It is essential to avoid viewing such imperatives through an apolitical and ahistorical lens, especially in the context of conquest and colonialism, and to critically examine the violence committed in the name of spiritual salvation and civilization and to question other hegemonic assumptions and processes in different periods (Andreotti, 2011; Grain & Lund, 2016; Mignolo, 2000). In current times, the Catholic Church is seen as one of the largest charitable organizations in the United States (Forbes,

2016). In relation to this, Catholic institutions of higher education in the twenty-first century tend to have, within their core values and missions, prominent statements about the need for students to enter the world with skills for ethical conduct and compassionate service. How these institutions choose to develop such skills in students vary based on the religious order with which a given college or university is affiliated; the approach is more focused on social justice in some cases, for example, and on the traditions of service and charity in others (Hughson, 2013; Wilcox & King, 2000). Completely independent of any particular order, USD's initial articulation of its commitment to the public good was more inscribed in the latter and, subsequently, manifested itself primarily through the promotion of volunteerism.

Consequently, the incipient efforts of service-learning at USD, which began in the 1980s, focused on traditional volunteerism. In fact, the institution established a Volunteer Resources Office partly in reaction to the actions of a longtime community leader and resident who encouraged the university administration to partner with organizations in the neighborhood, such as schools, community centers, and health facilities, in order to improve the quality of life for youth and address other local needs (R. Smith, personal communication, March 4, 2017). Many residents of the neighborhood tended to express the concern that the relationship with the university was mainly "transactional." Students, faculty, and staff patronized some of the local businesses, but the overall perception of residents was that the urban core was primarily a passageway through which the university community members commuted to and from campus. However, the gradual recognition emerged that only through conscious, deliberate actions could the "ivory tower on the hill" become activated to create equitable partnerships to help address some of the most pressing community-identified issues. Over the years, as the field of service-learning both developed and became more problematized at a national level (Butin, 2010; Jacoby, 2015; Saltmarsh & Zlotkowski, 2011; Stewart & Webster, 2011), the Volunteer Resources Office evolved into the Office of Community Service-Learning and was then transformed into the Center for Community Service-Learning. These transitions were essential for both the community and the university as those involved formed more intentional curricular and cocurricular partnerships. Two important factors made these changes possible: locally, the institution received various sources of funding, and nationally, the growth of community service-learning accelerated as not only a pedagogical practice but also a theoretically grounded discipline (Bringle & Hatcher, 1999; Jacoby & Associates, 2003).

The work of this center has expanded significantly through the years; it is estimated, for example, that now some 80% of undergraduate and graduate students at USD participate annually in some form of community engagement. More important, over the last two decades the center—which experienced an additional name change more recently to the Mulvaney Center for Community, Awareness and Social Action, emphasizing the shift from service to action—has greatly deepened its development of intentional partnerships. These partnerships link learning in the classroom to a greater understanding of the community through the practice and philosophy of coeducation (Cress, Stokamer, & Kaufman, 2015). This contributed to the university being designated as a community-engaged campus, as classified by the Carnegie Foundation. All these elements attest to the transformation from an earlier approach based on volunteerism to a more complex and integrated understanding and practice of curriculum-based community engagement aimed at deeper positive social change in collaboration with community partners.

Notwithstanding the aforementioned establishment and growth of community engagement at USD, in many ways the work of the center remains localized and does not encompass the entire university. Additionally, in spite of the center's development of a more critical approach to community engagement that merges with the work of social justice (Cipolle, 2010; Mitchell, 2008; Tinkler, Tinkler, Jagla, & Strait, 2016), for some campus members there is an ongoing perception that it operates within a service and volunteerism model. A clearly defined mechanism has been lacking for overcoming these misconceptions, for involving more individuals on campus in critical community engagement opportunities, and for encouraging more departments across disciplines to develop reciprocal partnerships with the local community. Similarly, the engaged scholarship produced at USD within different disciplines has focused largely on the impact of community engagement on student learning and development, and less on actual community impact: Camacho (2004); Ehrich, Ceranic, and Liu (2014); Guerrieri (2007); Liu (2016); Liu and Kelly (2010a, 2010b); Liu, Leppard, and Nayve (2012); Liu, Elliott, Loggins, and Nayve (2006); Sgoutas-Emch (2010); and Williams and Nunn (2016), among others. These are not necessarily problems unique to a given center for community engagement, but rather they constitute key challenges at the institutional level.

Broadening the Reach: Social Innovation and Changemaking

The relatively recent designation of USD as a Changemaker Campus by Ashoka U in 2011, accompanied by a discourse centered on the notion that anyone can create positive change in the world, has provided a platform from which to explore different challenges and issues through the lens of social innovation. Previously, the development of social entrepreneurship and social innovation at USD had been relatively gradual and limited primarily to the work of a handful of faculty members in the School of Business and a few other academic risk takers from other disciplines. However, with the Ashoka U designation, an imperative emerged to infuse social innovation across campus, which, consequently, has led to an examination of possibilities for implementation among multiple departments, programs, and schools seeking both curricular and cocurricular opportunities.

The introduction of the changemaker discourse at USD reflects broader tendencies. When community service-learning was growing as a discipline, the emergence of the social entrepreneur and innovator was gaining support at institutions of higher education (Butin, 2010). In this approach, there was an emphasis on the entrepreneur directly addressing community needs and seeking solutions to social ills (Robinson, 2006; Zahra, Gedajlovic, Neubaum, & Shulman, 2009). In response to this trend, a number of organizations began forming partnerships with colleges and universities to help nurture students, faculty, and staff to become the next generation of innovators. One such entity was the nonprofit organization Ashoka, founded in 1980, with the goal of empowering social entrepreneurs to address the world's most pressing issues. Later, the Ashoka U program was established in 2008 "to catalyze social innovation in higher education through a global network of change teams composed of entrepreneurial students, faculty, and community leaders" (Ashoka, n.d.). USD is now one of approximately 45 colleges and universities that have received the Changemaker Campus designation (Ashoka U, n.d.).

The transition to a changemaker identity was not without its issues. As the university adopted this new official identity, there was confusion around the ambiguous definition of the terminology and significant resistance to the way it was used for branding. USD was soon dominated by marketing schemes aimed at promoting the university as a changemaker institution. This new official discourse, based primarily on notions of social entrepreneurship and social innovation, appeared to eclipse much of the work in service-learning, community engagement, and relationship building that had been going on for decades. Rather than building on this strong foundation, the changemaker identity was often articulated as something distinct and unique. In addition, the discourse seemed to envision the community, whether locally or abroad, as a place of problems and deficits, which ran completely counter to asset-based approaches to community development (Kretzmann, 2010; Kretzmann & McKnight, 1993). In accordance with this initial changemaker vision, there was an urgent need for individuals with the right skill set and innovative thinking who would become the prime motors of social change. Many tensions arose around these notions, and there was and continues to be significant resistance on campus and in the community to what has been described more recently as "heropreneurship" (Papi-Thornton, 2016).

As a result of these tensions, the university has been reformulating the way that it employs the Ashoka U designation. Initially, in communications in admissions, marketing, and programming, the noun *changemaker* appeared consistently with the intention of inspiring students to become agents of change. No one defined the way one could become a changemaker in order to provide an open and inclusive space for a wide range of understandings of the term. However, this led to the aforementioned terminological ambiguity and the narrow focus on the need for an *individual's* innovation and commitment to change, frequently motivated by a "savior mentality" (Flaherty, 2016), which runs contrary to the call for humility (Grain & Lund, 2016) and ethical solidarity (Andreotti, 2007). Consequently, the approach at USD has now shifted from the individual, the changemaker, to the action of changemaking. This move is not mere semantics. By promoting the practice of changemaking, the emphasis shifts from *being* to *doing*, from identity (and, potentially, hubris) to the development and application of knowledge, skills, and values of social innovation and the collective work of social change. Similarly, in recent years, more changemaking initiatives and programs have been offered that focus on collaboration and a "team of teams" model.

The creation of the Changemaker Hub at USD was an important development that followed the initial Ashoka U designation more immediately. Instead of founding a new center or institute, the hub was conceptualized by a small group of faculty and administrators to act as an umbrella entity where individuals, the curriculum, and different organizations would converge in the diverse and multifaceted work of changemaking. Rather than seeking organizational autonomy, the focus has been on the shared ownership of the hub across campus. Many years after its creation, the hub continues to strive to encourage collaboration among academic units on campus to help expand the reach and capacity of the university to engage the community and promote social entrepreneurial and innovative projects.

In terms of faculty engagement, the hub revised its previous Changemaker Faculty Champions program and created a Changemaker Faculty Fellows Development Program in 2017–2018. While the former requested deans to nominate faculty as "changemaker champions," the Faculty Fellows initiative allows individuals to self-nominate through an application process. The result has been that the hub is able to collaborate with faculty who have a genuine interest in changemaking and social innovation. Moreover, the focus is shifted to a developmental approach and continuing the work into the future. The fellows meet routinely for a series of workshops on how to implement changemaking and social innovation in their teaching, research, and service commitments. This transformation of the program has proved worthwhile; the faculty participants have demonstrated not only a deeper understanding of USD's changemaking initiative but also enthusiasm to continue collaborating with the hub during the next academic year.

Through collaborations with other units on campus such as the Mulvaney Center for Community, Awareness and Social Action; the Center for Inclusion and Diversity; the Center for Educational Excellence; and University Ministry, the hub has created a number of initiatives to support the practice of changemaking. For example, the Social Change Corps (SCC) is a cocurricular program that provides students, working in groups of two to five, with the opportunity to learn about social issues that matter to them and to suggest ways to address these issues. The SCC encourages students to think creatively about issues that exist both on and off campus and to engage with community in ways that are meaningful, sustainable, and reciprocal.

In addition, the hub and its partners have also provided faculty development opportunities in which faculty engage in immersion experiences away from campus. These experiences allow faculty to learn about how different universities and communities are addressing important social, political, and economic issues. Equally important, these experiences create opportunities for faculty to collaborate in the classroom and through research projects. Since its inception, the hub has aspired to be a place on campus where faculty, students, and staff can connect with one another and work collaboratively on the issues that matter most to them. Although there is still much work to be done, the hub has made significant strides in the last few years to make these opportunities more accessible to the campus community as well as broader communities.

Finally, the tensions produced around the ambiguous notion of changemaking also led a group of faculty and staff at USD, sponsored by the Center for Educational Excellence, to design a model of change in an effort to develop a more inclusive and holistic framework for positive social change (Guerrieri & Sgoutas-Emch, 2016). This model has several guiding principles, including the imperative to work in ethical solidarity with others in an attempt to build more equitable, reciprocal, and democratic partnerships. This also means focusing on community assets while simultaneously deepening one's understanding of the complexity of issues through the exploration of historical, political, social, cultural, and other key aspects. Rising above the parameters and limitations of any single approach to working for the common good, ultimately, this group of faculty and staff attempted to disentangle broader questions of change and sought a more open and malleable framework that could help examine, enrich, and interconnect multiple modalities of engagement. Development, discussion, and implementation of the model became one of the ways that the university continues to work toward the integration of different entities and initiatives on campus.

Filling the Gaps: Anchor Institutions and Long-Term Social Change

As discussed previously, the university has a long history of deep connections with community partnerships that has evolved and expanded over the decades and has contributed to USD becoming one of only a handful of academic institutions that have received both the Carnegie Foundation's classification for community engagement and Ashoka U's Changemaker designation (Enos, 2015, 2016). USD's community engagement framework has operated in parallel with or been integrated into a wide range of community-centered activities that could be understood as anchor practices, such as providing landlord/tenant dispute resolution services, offering health screenings, staffing community health clinics, providing childhood development classes for parents, and promoting economic development and marketing training to small business owners, as a result of receiving a Community Outreach Partnership Center (COPC) grant in 1996 from the U.S. Department of Housing and Urban Development's Office of University Partnerships.

However, there are still many gaps in these relationships. In particular, most of these endeavors have arisen as part of a project-based curriculum or as components of programs that come and go depending on whether the course is offered during a given semester. Many of these programs are perceived as being led and organized by the university in service to the community, which inevitably reifies a power differential, both real and perceived, between the academic institution and the community (Taylor & Luter, 2013). Furthermore, the sustainability and adaptability of these partnerships are questionable. When a project is completed, what happens to the partnership? What resources or structures are in place to ensure the maintenance and growth of a particular program?

One approach to address these gaps, introduced by USD's new administration, consists of understanding the university as an anchor institution within the community. Many institutions across the nation are incorporating an anchor mission and embracing the responsibility for their economic, cultural, and social impact as they expand their commitment to the public good (Birch, Perry, & Taylor, 2013). As defined by Hodges and Dubbs (2012), this *anchor mission* consists of a commitment by the institutions to "consciously and strategically apply their long-term, place-based economic power, in combination with their human and intellectual resources, to better the welfare of the communities in which they reside" (pp. xix–xx). Anchor institutions are universities, schools, nonprofits, hospitals, and other organizations that are considered to be permanently located in a city or region. These organizations are rooted in their local communities and often have considerable resources. Accordingly, they have the potential to bring crucial and measurable benefits to their neighbors. However, it is essential to point out that, rather than conceiving of such benefits within a philanthropic service paradigm, the anchor institution movement promotes a model of democratic, reciprocal community-based partnerships and strong networks (Harris & Holley, 2016).

Although a campus-wide discourse of anchor institution framing is relatively new to USD, the concept and its related practices align well with the mission of the university, founded in a faith-based tradition, as well as with the long-term commitment to community engagement, evidenced by the aforementioned COPC grant, and the more recent incorporation of social innovation into the institution's identity. Ultimately, USD seeks to continue building long-term, interdependent, and sustainable partnerships with the surrounding community, and the partner organizations are seen as cocreators guiding the direction of social change. In this sense, the creation of the Linda Vista Anchor Institution Advisory Board—comprising leaders, residents, and practitioners committed to increasing the economic, cultural, and social health of the community—exemplifies the fact that the university is only one of many anchors in the community. Critical points of collaboration are community-identified issues, such as public health, education, food security, and economic development. These are key efforts that seek to respond to the need identified by the national Anchor Institution Task Force to deepen the alignment "across institutions, civic organizations, citizens, policy, foundations, and the private sector" in order to create a thick network of human and social capital to address "societal problems and to build an equitable society based on democracy, social justice and a commitment to place and community" (Taylor & Luter, 2013, p. 1).

The program called Impact Linda Vista Initiative (ILVI) is a concrete example that illustrates the integration of community engagement, social innovation, and anchor institution concepts. Informed by the aforementioned model of change, ILVI is a program that reflects efforts at USD to continue building bridges among different entities on campus, identify common causes, and collectively strengthen relationships specifically in the Linda Vista community. ILVI is funded primarily by a grant that the Changemaker Hub has received annually from a local bank to promote innovative and sustainable initiatives in the neighborhood by supporting collaboration between community partners and USD students and faculty. Initially implemented in 2014 with a strong emphasis on locating innovation in the community and producing deliverables, ILVI has transformed significantly in a short period because of the strong collaboration between the Changemaker Hub and the Mulvaney Center for Community, Awareness and Social Action.

After examining the initiative through the lens of the aforementioned model of change, the focus shifted to deeper and more intentional relationship building with partners. This is manifested at multiple levels: (a) one faculty member and one community member are invited to implement and manage the initiative as codirectors, (b) the call for proposals is distributed to both faculty and community partners each semester, (c) the initial selection process is based on cocreation sessions with faculty applicants and community partners, and (d) monetary support is provided for both faculty and partners. In this sense, ILVI is one example of how USD is assuming—albeit to a relatively limited degree—the roles of *facilitator* (distributing real economic resources across numerous organizations) and *convener* (helping to bring together different organizations, sectors, and disciplines to address community concerns), using here the anchor mission terminology of Hodges and Dubbs (2012). This approach highlights the importance of community knowledge and assets, as we recognize partners as coeducators in USD students' learning process; the actual course-based projects are cocreated through the initial sessions. This exemplifies many of the components contained in the model of change—first, the focus on community relationships, the collective determination of mission, values, and purpose. Similarly, the model emphasizes deep learning in which wisdom and multiple ways of knowing beyond the walls of the academy are equally valued, and participants understand knowledge as a process, not a product, which speaks to an approach that seeks to deconstruct hegemonic structures of knowledge production (Andreotti, 2011).

In addition to the explicit effort to work in ethical solidarity with community partners, ILVI strives to cultivate sustainable and long-term positive social change, which requires the exploration of issues from multiple perspectives and a transdisciplinary lens. The model of change includes the components of interdependence (which recognizes the interconnections of human action, society, and the natural world) and synthesis (which strives for the innovative unification of multiple perspectives, disciplines, and resources while simultaneously exploring complexity and respecting difference) (Guerrieri & Sgoutas-Emch, 2016). Each semester of the grant year, all participants—including both the current and incoming cohorts—convene in order to describe their initiatives, share ideas, and determine potential connections. The partners have included, among others, two community centers, a kindergarten readiness network, an elementary school, a middle school, a high school, a charter school, a teen center, the local branch of the public library, several community gardens, a farmers' market, the San Diego police department, and a health clinic with multiple branches across the city. The faculty participants have come from numerous departments and academic units on campus, at both the undergraduate and graduate levels: College of Arts and Sciences (biology; communication studies; languages, cultures and literatures; mathematics; psychological sciences; sociology; theater; and theology and religious studies), School of Business, School of Engineering, School of Leadership and Education Sciences, School of Nursing, and School of Peace Studies.

By engaging this wide array of academic departments, disciplines, and community organizations, ILVI reflects the model of change's inclusion of structures and systems as key capacities for long-term social change, which cannot be achieved without the examination of systemic conditions and structures that either inhibit or facilitate change. In this sense, in spite of the limitation of a one-year grant renewed annually, actual participation in ILVI is framed around long-term thinking and continuity planning, thereby attempting to avoid the one-semester project mentality. Similarly, all participants are encouraged to reflect on mechanisms and strategies for improving their initiatives and building on the work realized in future semesters and years. The model of change also highlights the coexistence of situatedness and multiple levels of convergence in the work of change (from the personal and local to the regional, national, and global) (Brickell & Datta, 2011).

Some understand social innovation as a "novel solution to a social problem that is more effective, efficient, sustainable, or just than existing solutions and for which the value created accrues primarily to society as a whole rather than private individuals" (Phills, Deiglmeier, & Miller, 2008, p. 39). The novelty of ILVI, in part, consists of the way it creates overlapping networks of collaboration: direct cooperation among different centers on campus; the interdisciplinary cross-fertilization produced among academic units; and the alignment of endeavors from the public, private, and nonprofit sectors. In addition, it aligns with the anchor mission by strengthening democratic and reciprocal relationships in which community partners are cocreators, and it includes direct resource allocation.

Lessons Learned and Key Guidelines

The preceding institutional narrative does not present a teleological view on a perceived evolution from charity to social justice, but rather a reflection on some of the key transformations, challenges, and opportunities that have emerged over the last four decades in the context of USD's commitment to civic engagement. The three major developments highlighted in this case study—community engagement, social innovation, and anchor institution mission—not only reflect national trends at given historical moments but also continue to function simultaneously and in parallel with other practices and approaches to the civic mission of the university. As the institute continues the work of social justice education, the lessons learned serve as five general guidelines. They are discussed in the following section.

Guideline 1: Critical Self-Reflection at the Institutional Level

What is the balance in the institution's undergraduate education among the liberal arts (with intellectual exploration and inquiry across the arts, humanities, natural sciences, and social sciences at the heart of students' academic formation), civic learning, and career preparation? What are the decision-making processes at the university for strategic planning, the development of major initiatives, the reorganization of units and leadership, the (re)allocation of resources, and the uses of and changes to the buildings and physical space of the campus? How transparent and democratic are these processes and what forms of consultation take place with different constituencies and stakeholders? How strong and active are the shared-governance structures and mechanisms of the university? To what degree do the different units on campus tend to function as independent and autonomous entities, rather than as integrated parts of a larger organization? Similarly, are communication and collaboration ingrained practices in the institutional culture and not just an afterthought or rare occurrence? How well does the official discourse of the university align with varying perceptions of its collective identity? Does branding, marketing, and public relations messaging drive the institutional direction, or, rather, does the work on the ground drive this, by the teaching and learning, research, scholarship, and creative work? In what ways can the university's policies, procedures, and practices be improved to avoid contributing to the multiple faces of oppression—exploitation, marginalization, powerlessness, cultural imperialism, and violence (Young, 1990)—on campus, in the community, and beyond?

The university community must continually pose these questions, especially decision-making individuals and groups at all levels of administration and leadership. Self-reflection will potentially move toward critical self-reflection as the institution examines power differentials, structures, and practices that oppress as well as previously unquestioned norms and status quo assumptions (Kiely, 2015). Clearly, this critical reflection must result in the implementation of material changes and also continue as an ongoing process.

Guideline 2: Multiple Understandings of and Approaches to Social Change

When long-term practitioners of community engagement enter into dialogue with advocates of social entrepreneurship, the wide range of understandings of what constitutes civic engagement and what forms social justice education should take in the university quickly comes to the forefront. The aforementioned model of change designed by a group of faculty and staff at USD takes into account this diversity of approaches and in some ways builds on Morton's (1995) argument that different paradigms of service-learning—translated in the present context as the multiple paradigms of social change—do not necessarily follow a developmental continuum but can and do coexist. Similarly, the model of change complements the Social Change Wheel, created by the Minnesota Campus Compact (n.d.), and Enos's (2015) "social change toolbox," (p. 74) among other multifaceted frameworks. Clearly, some tensions can and usually do emerge among the different approaches, especially when they are informed by different ideological positions and worldviews. This should not be seen in a negative light but, rather, as a potential catalyst for deepening the work with a more critical and comprehensive perspective.

Guideline 3: Collaboration Among Different Entities on Campus

The rapid growth of social entrepreneurship, with its emphasis on innovation, can easily lead to the creation of a competitive environment or reliance on a corporate-type mentality. Often, the most visible presence of social entrepreneurship on campus may be the competitions in which teams or individuals strive to come up with the most innovative ideas for change or social venture plans (Meyskens & Auch, 2014). This competitive framework, in which members of the same team foster collaboration, is replicated on campus when different units, such as centers, institutes, and academic programs, must compete for limited university resources. Precisely for this reason, it is essential to develop specific mechanisms and spaces for collaboration at multiple levels in the institution, especially those designed to enhance the diversity of participants, perspectives, and approaches to social change and civic learning.

Asset mapping and goal alignment are key tools to identifying collaborators to create meaningful initiatives. A recent example of this at USD was the creation of a professional learning community (PLC) dedicated to exploring the implementation of the six pathways of Envisioning 2024, the university's new strategic plan. The goal of this PLC, comprising 12 faculty and staff members from different areas on campus, was to dive deeper into the vision of the various pathways, including what it means to be an anchor institution, to practice changemaking, and to be a diverse and inclusive institution. Most important here, the PLC was made possible through the combined resources of the Changemaker Hub; the Center for Educational Excellence; the Center for Inclusion and Diversity; and the Mulvaney Center for Community, Awareness and Social Action. Each unit contributed to the resources and tools necessary to help support this initiative in a meaningful and holistic fashion that is often not possible with just one center or unit. Many members of this learning community continue to collaborate on different projects and now form an extended community of practice.

There are additional mechanisms and spaces at USD in which collaboration on social issues among different units across campus has grown. These include the Humanities Center; University Galleries; and the USD Just Read! Program, sponsored by the Center for Educational Excellence. Likewise, a Faculty Council on Community Engagement has been created with members from multiple areas with the explicit charge of strengthening the network of communication and collaboration. Finally, the university is in the process of implementing a web-based platform that will serve to document and connect community engagement activities carried out by units across campus. This platform will also be used to collect data on the activities.

Guideline 4: Integration at the Institutional Level

USD is currently undergoing the implementation of long-term institutional strategic planning, initiated by the top administration, and its civic action plan, which stems from the university's commitment to Campus Compact's (2016) 30th Anniversary Action Statement of Presidents and Chancellors. The former, which was approved by the board of trustees, explicitly unites the three areas discussed in this chapter—community engagement, social innovation, and anchor institution strategies—into six interconnected pathways: anchor institution, practicing changemaking, access and inclusion, engaged scholarship, care for our common home, and liberal arts education for the twenty-first century. The university's civic action plan, in turn, was crafted in a way that interwove it into the broader strategic planning with the intention of integrating it into the institution's road map for the next decade. This integration speaks to many of the "lessons learned" about the governance of the university as an anchor institution. These lessons range from "on-the-ground projects and practices" to securing the support of the leadership at the highest level, and from the convergence of the core academic mission of the institution to harnessing "the power of the institution's role as an economic engine" (Harkavy, Hartley, Hodges, Sorrento, & Weeks, 2014, p. 114). Integration at the institutional level is an ongoing and long-term endeavor that encompasses the core curriculum, the living learning communities, and many other areas and aspects of the university. It must be acknowledged that this process of integration is still aspirational in many ways and requires significant coordination and collaboration in order to advance.

Guideline 5: Community Partnerships and Relationships

The emergence and growth of social entrepreneurship education and initiatives, on the one hand, provide new ways of conceptualizing and implementing social change and, on the other hand, pose potential risks. Often leaders add an additional layer of academic/administrative bureaucracy to manage these efforts, which contributes to the university's administrative bloat. Additionally, there is duplication of parallel ongoing efforts within the university that remain separated because of a lack of integration between and among the programs—hence, the previous guideline. Finally, a growing zeal for going out into the community to implement different initiatives—sometimes with little or no knowledge of existing institutional relationships—can overburden community partners and potentially damage those relationships. This guideline focuses precisely on the nature of the community partnerships and relationships, which undoubtedly constitute the core of any engagement off campus.

We must define the terminology used to conceptualize the connections and interactions between the university and the community organizations. Bringle, Clayton, and Price (2009) marked a clear distinction between *community partnerships* and *relationships*; whereas the latter is a "general and broad term to refer to all types of interactions between persons," the former constitutes a more formalized relationship that "possess[es] three particular qualities: closeness, equity, and integrity" (p. 3). Aligned with these notions of closeness, equity, and integrity, USD's Mulvaney Center for Community, Awareness and Social Action has historically understood partnerships as relational, trust based, and deeply transformational for both parties. However, more recently the center has also embarked on the process of solidifying and enhancing the university's partnership infrastructure, partly because of the implementation of the anchor institution mission. A new position was created, the director of neighborhood and community engaged partnerships, which not only functions as a liaison between the town and gown but also serves to develop memorandums of understanding (MOUs) that articulate the mutually agreed-on expectations for both the partner and the university. Such MOUs serve to acknowledge, explore, and develop complex and multifaceted partnerships that can reflect and manage the convergence of social entrepreneurship and community engagement. Additionally, the MOUs can help establish some clearer parameters for measuring the impact of partnerships through continual revisiting and dialoguing about those connections. As Martin and Crossland (2017) noted, it is essential that "this process defines clear goals, creates accountability, and considers the opportunity for equitable leadership" (p. 172).

Both partnerships and relationships are fluid and can take many different shapes over time. Partner organizations must be respected as autonomous and independent entities driven by their own missions, objectives, and decision-making processes. Accordingly, while transformational campus-community relationships may be an ideal to pursue, it is important to understand that sometimes "transactional, mutually-beneficial levels of relationship are satisfying and perhaps appropriate" (Clayton, Bringle, Senor, Huq, & Morrison, 2010, p. 18). This approach explicitly seeks to recognize the power differentials that may exist and the political aspects involved and, accordingly, to consider them as the partnership is developed or deepened. Related to this idea, Saltmarsh, Hartley, and Clayton (2009) noted the need to explore the political dimension in the work of civic engagement; they posit that, in the context of community-university partnerships, politics are understood "through explicit awareness and experiencing of patterns of power that are present in the relationship between the university and the community" (p. 11). In light of this, Saltmarsh and colleagues (2009) emphasized the key role of "democratic" (p. 11) civic engagement, which integrates the political dimension into the work and is based on reciprocity, an asset-based understanding of community, and the cocreation and multidirectional flow of knowledge, among other aspects.

The nuances of community partnerships and relationships—and of how they are interwoven—are at the foundation of the civic mission of the university. The formalized agreements that define expectations and responsibilities serve a key function in strengthening partnerships. However, relationships, both formal and informal, are what make such agreements possible and on which their implementation and longevity depend. A firm commitment to democratic, equitable, and reciprocal relationships and partnerships must also be matched by an understanding of their changing nature. Guided by these principles, ultimately, the university aspires to the transformational, from the personal to the societal level.

Present Challenges and New Directions

The greatest dilemma within the field of service-learning is that it "has the capacity to exacerbate inequality when done poorly, and to be a promising equalizing force when done well" (Grain & Lund, 2016, p. 48). This dilemma, clearly, also encompasses the objectives of social innovation and anchor institution strategies. As one community resident reflected on the notion of *anchor institutions*, she expressed a sentiment that many overstudied community members often feel when a university agenda is perceived to overtake community-identified goals: "An anchor is something that gets dropped on people's heads" (Rutheiser, 2012, p. xi). Indeed, as Harkavy (2016) has recently written, it is questionable whether any urban university has yet fulfilled the fundamental criteria to become a truly engaged university. Nonetheless, at USD the implementation of anchor development strategies—interwoven with the work of community engagement and initiatives in social innovation—is providing a key component of the institution's ongoing path to strengthening and sustaining community partnerships that, ultimately, seek to improve significantly the quality of life in communities.

There are certainly many ongoing challenges: How can we assess more effectively the impact on the community, in both qualitative and quantitative terms? How can the university harness and integrate a wide range of approaches to preparing students for community engagement and active citizenship across disciplines, academic units, and fields of study? Similarly, how can the institution foster a deeper and more meaningful cohesion of the students' academic formation in the liberal arts, their preparation for the professions, and the long-term work of social justice? This chapter emphasizes that by deeply integrating community engagement, social innovation, and anchor institution strategies, colleges and universities may reinterpret and reimagine their institutional missions while maintaining the liberal arts education at the heart.

References

Andreotti, V. (2007). An ethical engagement with the Other: Spivak's ideas on education. *Critical Literacy: Theories and Practice, 1*(1), 69–79. Retrieved from http://www.criticalliteracyjournal.org

Andreotti, V. (2011). *Actionable postcolonial theory in education.* New York, NY: Palgrave Macmillan.

Ashoka. (n.d.). *About.* Retrieved from https://www.ashoka.org/en

Ashoka U. (n.d.). *Home.* Retrieved from http://ashokau.org

Birch, E., Perry, D. C., & Taylor, H. L. (2013). Universities as anchor institutions. *Journal of Higher Education Outreach and Engagement, 17*(3), 7–15.

Brickell, K., & Datta, A. (Eds.). (2011). *Translocal geographies: Spaces, places, connections.* Abingdon, Oxon, UK: Ashgate.

Bringle, R. G., Clayton, P. H., & Price, M. (2009). Partnerships in service learning and civic engagement. *Partnerships: A Journal of Service Learning & Civic Engagement, 1*(1), 1–20.

Bringle, R. G., & Hatcher, J. A. (1999, Spring). Reflection in service learning: Making meaning or experience. *Evaluation/Reflection,* 23. Retrieved from http://digitalcommons.unomaha.edu/slceeval/23

Butin, D. W. (2010). *Service learning in theory and practice: The future of community engagement in higher education.* New York, NY: Palgrave Macmillan.

Camacho, M. M. (2004). Power and privilege: Community service learning in Tijuana. *Michigan Journal of Community Service Learning, 10*(3), 31–42.

Campus Compact. (2016). *30th anniversary action statement of presidents and chancellors.* Retrieved from http://compact.org/actionstatement/statement/

Cipolle, S. B. (2010). *Service-learning and social justice: Engaging students in social change.* Plymouth, UK: Rowman & Littlefield.

Clayton, P. H., Bringle, R. G., Senor, B., Huq, J., & Morrison, M. (2010). Differentiating and assessing relationships in service-learning and civic engagement: Exploitative, transactional, or transformational. *Michigan Journal of Community Service Learning, 16*(2), 5–21.

Cress, C. M., Stokamer, S. T., & Kaufman, J. P. (2015). *Community partner guide to campus collaborations: Enhance your community by becoming a co-educator with colleges and universities*. Sterling, VA: Stylus.

Ehrich, K., Ceranic, T., & Liu, J. (2014). Business unusual: Transforming business school curricula through community engagement. *Metropolitan Universities Journal, 25*, 111–124.

Enos, S. L. (2015). *Service-learning and social entrepreneurship in higher education: A pedagogy of social change*. New York, NY: Palgrave Macmillan.

Enos, S. L. (2016). Independent, coexisting, collaborating? How institutions are organizing their efforts for social impact. *Diversity & Democracy, 19*(3). Retrieved from http://www.aacu.org/diversitydemocracy/2016/summer/enos

Flaherty, J. (2016). *No more heroes: Grassroots challenges to the savior mentality*. Oakland, CA: AK Press.

Forbes. (2016). *The 100 largest U.S. charities*. Retrieved from https://www.forbes.com/top-charities/list/#tab:rank

Grain, K. M., & Lund, D. E. (2016). The *social justice turn*: Cultivating "critical hope" in an age of despair. *Michigan Journal of Community Service Learning, 23*(1), 45–59.

Guerrieri, K. (2007). Leer y escribir la frontera: Language, literature, and community engagement in the San Diego-Tijuana borderlands. In S. Danielson & A. F. Fallon (Eds.), *Community-based learning and the work of literature* (pp. 154–179). Bolton, MA: Anker.

Guerrieri, K., & Sgoutas-Emch, S. (2016). Immersions in global equality and social justice: A model of change. *Engaging Pedagogies in Catholic Higher Education, 2*(1), 1–9. Retrieved from https://digitalcommons.stmarys-ca.edu/epiche/vol2/iss1/4/

Harkavy, I. (2016). Engaging urban universities as anchor institutions for health equity. *American Journal of Public Health, 106*(12), 2155–2157.

Harkavy, I., Hartley, M., Hodges, R. A., Sorrento, A., & Weeks, J. (2014). Effective governance of a university as an anchor institution. *Leadership and Governance in Higher Education, 2*, 97–116.

Harris, M., & Holley, K. (2016). Universities as anchor institutions: Economic and social potential for urban development. In M. B. Paulsen (Ed.), *Higher education: Handbook of theory and research* (pp. 393–439). New York, NY: Springer International.

Hodges, R. A., & Dubbs, S. (2012). *The road half traveled: University engagement at a crossroads*. East Lansing: Michigan State University Press.

Hughson, T. (2013). *Connecting Jesus to social justice: Classical Christology and public theology*. New York, NY: Rowman & Littlefield.

Jacoby, B. (2015). *Service-learning essentials: Questions, answers, and lessons learned*. San Francisco, CA: Jossey-Bass.

Jacoby, B., & Associates. (2003). *Building partnerships for service-learning.* San Francisco, CA: Jossey-Bass.

Kaczor, C. (2007). *Seven principles of Catholic social teaching.* Retrieved from https://www.catholic.com/magazine/print-edition/seven-principles-of-catholic-social-teaching

Kiely, R. (2015, October 13). *Considering critical reflection.* Campus Compact. Retrieved from https://compact.org/resource-posts/criticalreflection/

Kretzmann, J. P. (2010). Asset-based strategies for building resilient communities. In J. W. Reich, A. Zautra, & J. S. Hall (Eds.), *Handbook of adult resilience* (pp. 484–495). New York, NY: Guilford Press.

Kretzmann, J. P., & McKnight, J. L. (1993). *Building communities from the inside out: A path toward finding and mobilizing a community's assets.* Evanston, IL: Center for Urban Affairs and Policy Research, Northwestern University.

Liu, J. (2016). Reflections on skipping stones to diving deep: The process of immersion as a practice. *Engaging Pedagogies in Catholic Higher Education, 2*(1), 1–7. Retrieved from https://digitalcommons.stmarys-ca.edu/cgi/viewcontent.cgi?article=1011&context=epiche

Liu, J., Elliott, E., Loggins, J., & Nayve, C. (2006). Toward common unity: From silent to more equitable partnerships. *Metropolitan Universities Journal: An International Forum, 17*(1), 104–115.

Liu, J., & Kelly, D. P. (2010a). "Democracy is hard"/"Democracy is messy." *Journal for Civic Commitment, 16*(1), 1–13.

Liu, J., & Kelly, D. P. (2010b). Just a community organizer: Community/campus connections through organizing. *Metropolitan Universities Journal: An International Forum, 20*(3), 47–60.

Liu, J., Leppard, E., & Nayve, C. (2012). "Nothing about us without us is for us": Civic engagement through consensus and commitment. *Journal for Civic Commitment, 19,* 1–20.

Martin, L., & Crossland, S. (2017). High-quality community-campus partnerships: Approaches and competencies. In L. Dostilio (Ed.), *The community engagement professional in higher education: A competency model for an emerging field* (pp. 161–178). Boston, MA: Campus Compact.

Meyskens, M., & Auch, N. (2014). Value creation at the individual, venture and societal levels of analyses through social venture competitions. In B. Honig, J. Lampel, & I. Drori (Eds.), *Theory and empirical research in social entrepreneurship* (pp. 256–291). Northampton, MA: Edward Elgar.

Mignolo, W. (2000). *Local histories/global designs: Coloniality, subaltern knowledges, and border thinking.* Princeton, NJ: Princeton University Press.

Minnesota Campus Compact. (n.d.) *Social Change Wheel.* Retrieved from https://mncampuscompact.org/what-we-do/publications/social-change-wheel/

Mitchell, T. D. (2008). Traditional vs. critical service-learning: Engaging the literature to differentiate two models. *Michigan Journal of Community Service Learning, 14*(2), 50–65.

Papi-Thornton, D. (2016, February 23). Tackling heropreneurship: Why we need to move from "the social entrepreneur" to social impact. *Stanford Social Innovation Review*. Retrieved from https://ssir.org/articles/entry/tackling_heropreneurship

Phills, J. A., Deiglmeier, K., & Miller, D. T. (2008, Fall). Rediscovering social innovation. *Stanford Social Innovation Review, 6*(4), 33–43.

Robinson, J. (2006). Navigating social and institutional barriers to markets: How social entrepreneurs identify and evaluate opportunities. In J. Mair, J. Robinson, & K. Hockerts (Eds.), *Social entrepreneurship* (pp. 95–120). New York, NY: Palgrave Macmillan.

Rutheiser, C. (2012). Forward. In R. A. Hodges & S. Dubbs (Eds.), *The road half traveled: University engagement* (p. xi). East Lansing: Michigan State University Press.

Saltmarsh, J., Hartley, M., & Clayton, P. (2009). *Democratic Engagement White Paper*. New England Resource Center for Higher Education. Retrieved from https://repository.upenn.edu/cgi/viewcontent.cgi?article=1252&context=gse_pubs

Saltmarsh, J., & Zlotkowski, E. (2011). *Higher education and democracy: Essays on service learning and civic engagement.* Philadelphia, PA: Temple University Press.

Sgoutas-Emch, S. A. (2010). Is that politics in my health care? Implementing political engagement in a health psychology course to increase student awareness. *Journal for Civic Commitment, 14*(1), 1-11.

Stewart, T., & Webster, N. (Eds.). (2011). *Problematizing service-learning: Critical perspectives for development and action.* Charlotte, NC: Information Age.

Taylor, H. L., & Luter, G. (2013). *Anchor institutions: An interpretative review essay.* Anchor Institution Task Force, University at Buffalo. Retrieved from https://community-wealth.org/content/anchor-institutions-interpretive-review-essay

Tinkler, A., Tinkler, B., Jagla, V., & Strait, J. (Eds.). (2016). *Service-learning to advance social justice in a time of radical inequality.* Charlotte, NC: Information Age.

United States Conference of Catholic Bishops. (n.d.). *Sharing Catholic social teaching: Challenges and directions.* Retrieved from http://www.usccb.org/beliefs-and-teachings/what-we-believe/catholic-social-teaching/sharing-catholic-social-teaching-challenges-and-directions.cfm

University of San Diego. (n.d.). *Mission, vision and values.* Retrieved from https://www.sandiego.edu/about/mission-vision-values.php

Wilcox, J., & King, I. (Eds.). (2000). *Enhancing religious identity: Best practices from Catholic campuses.* Washington, DC: Georgetown University Press.

Williams, J. M., & Nunn, L. M. (2016). Immersive practices: Dilemmas of power and privilege in community engagement with students in a rural South African village. *Engaging Pedagogies in Catholic Higher Education, 2*(1), 1–8. Retrieved from https://digitalcommons.stmarys-ca.edu/cgi/viewcontent.cgi?article=1009&context=epiche

Young, I. M. (1990). *Justice and the politics of difference*. Princeton, NJ: Princeton University Press.

Zahra, S. A., Gedajlovic, E., Neubaum, D. O., & Shulman, J. M. (2009). A typology of social entrepreneurs: Motives, search processes and ethical challenges. *Journal of Business Venturing, 24*(5), 519–532.

PART FOUR

MOVING THE FIELD FORWARD

Chapter Seven

SOCIAL INNOVATION AND CIVIC ENGAGEMENT

A Critical Praxis for Engagement in Higher Education

Cadence Willse, prabhdeep singh kehal, and Mathew B. Johnson

Since the 1960s and 1970s, colleges and universities have institutionalized a civic and social focus into their programmatic planning for students. Two parallel trajectories have approached student engagement in paradigmatically distinct ways (see Figure 7.1). The first trajectory began with student engagement as service-learning or community service, transformed service-learning into civic engagement, and has now arrived at democratic civic engagement as the organizing framework on college and university campuses. The second trajectory also started with student engagement but now focuses on the role of entrepreneurs and how they produce social benefit through social entrepreneurship and eventually social innovation. While some scholars call for a bridging of social innovation and civic engagement (Scobey, 2015), we argue that, rather than collapsing the trajectories into one path, both approaches to engagement will benefit from a discussion of power relations and shared context. Through these discussions, practitioners and scholars will arrive at the framework of democratic civic engagement. We argue that social innovation would benefit from this same attention, and we call this new framework *democratic social innovation.*

These two trajectories approach student engagement differently because of fundamental differences in the value proposition. The public good trajectory defines *social value* as the labor college and university members contribute to their communities, and the *private value* is for the student, college, and university because it aligns with their social mission. With a focus on aligning student engagement with its stated public missions, institutions of higher education first channeled student engagement through service-learning in this trajectory. In contrast, the market-based trajectory defines the *social value* as the product an entrepreneur produces for the community, whether or not it is necessarily needed by the community; the *private value* is financial gain for the investor and the entrepreneur. The market-based trajectory's emphasis on private value represents the viewpoint that entrepreneurs are not agents of change but exploiters of change (Drucker, 1985). In this view, investors and donors see colleges and universities engaged in knowledge production and identify untapped opportunities for private value generation. The value propositions in the two trajectories progress toward a greater awareness: Because private value had been prioritized over the social value, a paradigm shift was necessary to alter the value proposition. In this way, what we refer to as paradigms pushes the public good and market-based trajectories toward a more equitable distribution in the value proposition, not necessarily a more equal one.

As colleges and universities invested more in student engagement, scholars and practitioners studied engagement in practice and raised concerns regarding college and university engagement with communities. The initial critiques centered on the impact that higher education was having on their communities and the extent to which partnerships were reciprocal. Then, critiques became increasingly attentive to the power relations embedded within partnerships, and how these partnerships may be exploiting the shared political and economic context between institutions of higher education and their communities. These critiques reached a critical mass in two separate moments, each demanding a change in praxis. We refer to these moments as paradigms.

First, to better understand the paradigm of impact and reciprocity with the local, state, national, and global communities, institutions transformed their service programs to be more civically and community oriented. The transformation arose from practitioners' concerns that students were extracting personal value from impoverished and exploited communities without ensuring mutual benefit. Over time, practitioners realized that solely identifying impact and reciprocity was not enough and a more structural and historical conception of engagement was necessary.

Second, the current paradigm recognizes the power relations and shared context among students, colleges and universities, and the communities with which they engage. When we refer to shared context, we mean the shared economic and political context between colleges and universities and their community partners. As a result, practitioners and scholars push institutions to consider their engagement as part of a deliberative and democratic society. In other words, the second paradigm calls for an epistemological decentering of the university and for innovators to recognize and create avenues for collaborative knowledge generation with the community such that social value is truly prioritized in an equitable fashion. While these two paradigms impacted both trajectories of student engagement, each trajectory responded in different ways. Figure 7.1 offers a summary graphic of these trajectories and paradigm shifts.

The vertical arrows in Figure 7.1 represent the paradigms, and the horizontal arrows represent the trajectories over time. We conceptualize these two trajectories as forward moving and cumulative. Concerns around impact and reciprocity were pervasive in the field of higher education, resulting in the movement from social entrepreneurship to social innovation, and from service-learning to civic engagement, marking institutional

Figure 7.1 The market-based (top) and public good–based (bottom) trajectories of student engagement.

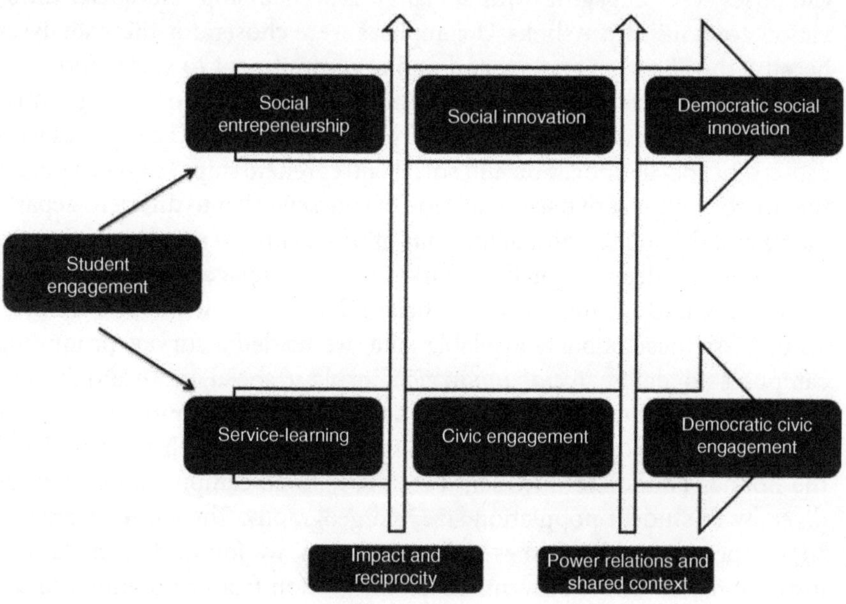

shifts in theory and practice. Similarly, because of ineffective institutional responses to the challenges presented to student engagement in paradigm 1, criticisms emerged around power relations and shared context. These criticisms coalesced in what we refer to as paradigm 2, marking the shift from civic engagement to democratic civic engagement and the potential shift from social innovation to democratic social innovation. We do not presume that these shifts in trajectory happened simultaneously, as Figure 7.1 may imply, because institutions' responses varied over time. Figure 7.1 simply displays that, as approaches to student engagement progressed, the same critiques were applied in both trajectories.

In this chapter, we describe the parallel trajectories of student engagement and trace their development over time. We critically review the literature on these trajectories, identifying how research on student engagement responds to the paradigm shifts, focusing on impact, reciprocity, power relations, and shared context. We focus on the following empirical research questions: (a) How do institutions of higher education engage with social innovation and social entrepreneurship through academic programming? (b) Are *social entrepreneurship* and *social innovation* defined as distinct concepts? (c) To what extent do campuses combine social entrepreneurship, social innovation, and civic engagement, and to what extent are conceptualizations distinct?

To address these questions, we collected publicly available course- and department-level data from Ashoka U campuses to assess how units on campuses were engaging with social entrepreneurship and social innovation academically. Ashoka U campuses were chosen for these analyses because they have an explicit and public commitment to social entrepreneurship and social innovation. In addition, we collected definitions, mission statements, and statements of purpose from Ashoka U campuses with centers for social innovation and social entrepreneurship. The data suggest that there is hyperactive segmentation of coursework into different departments and disciplines, and definitions of *social entrepreneurship* and *social innovation* are deeply rooted in market-based language. These definitions are less focused on mutually beneficial relationships with communities. To buttress these publicly available data, we fielded a survey, prompting campuses to define *social innovation*, explain social innovation's connection to community engagement, and list curricular and cocurricular offerings related to social innovation. In collaboration with Ashoka U and the Bonner Foundation, we sent the survey to 26 campuses, selected for diversity in student population size and geography. The survey yielded a 50% response rate. With these sources of data, we found that the lack of institutional guidance prevents social innovation from responding to the current paradigmatic shift focused on power relations and shared context.

Institutional frameworks that encourage attention to power relations and shared context would enrich campuses' programming on social entrepreneurship and social innovation, while also providing connections across curricular offerings rather than the observed hypersegmentation.

We argue that if social innovation were to meet the call of power relations and shared context, the trajectory from social entrepreneurship to social innovation would progress into democratic social innovation rather than recede to social entrepreneurship. In response to concerns around impact and reciprocity in their partnerships, institutions attempted to equalize private and social value generation, shifting the value proposition and moving from social entrepreneurship to social innovation. Yet, without attention to power relations and shared context, a more equal distribution of private and social value generation does not mitigate the underlying tension of the entrepreneur's exploitation of societal disadvantage (Drucker, 1985). Democratic social innovation, which we discuss at length in this chapter, decenters the epistemological core of the entrepreneur, innovator, or expert and centers the community in the coproduction of social value and change. Rather than fall into a paternalistic or neocolonial trap of prescribing the means and terms of change for marginalized communities, democratic social innovation calls on individuals and organizations to bring their skills to the community and allows the community to define the problem and terms of change and development.

Social innovation risks further exploiting disadvantaged communities by failing to embrace how a focus on impact and reciprocity would maintain, rather than challenge, existing power dynamics.. The Carnegie Community Engagement Classification, we argue, provides an architecture and approach for benchmarking and tracking progress toward symbiotic relationships with the community and begins a process of consistent evaluation. With this additional focus on the institution's role in social innovation, the classification reconceptualizes community-based work for social innovation (O'Meara & Rice, 2005). The classification articulates student engagement for a social good, encouraging colleges and universities to commit to an explicit conception of a social good. In doing so, institutions can assess the depth of their commitment to societal benefits and justice.

Defining the Trajectories of the Parallel Pathways

After the civil rights movement, campuses began promoting a more systematic engagement of community in the 1980s (Saltmarsh, 2005). In this chapter, we identify two parallel trajectories emerging from this institutional response: one inspired by public good–based logic and one motivated by market-based logic. The public good–based trajectory moves from service-learning activities and engagements with community toward civic engagement as a new paradigm and ultimately arrives at democratic civic engagement. In contrast, the market-based trajectory applies entrepreneurial techniques to social problems, emphasizing social entrepreneurship and ultimately social innovation as tools for social change. In addition, market-based approaches to social change have not grappled with the concepts of power relations and shared context in creating meaningful community partnerships. In this section, we define these terms and their relations to each other along their trajectories as they respond to two paradigmatic changes that occurred in student cocurricular activities.

Paradigm One's Effect on Trajectories

The first paradigmatic shift, which we call *impact and reciprocity*, was focused on identifying the civic outcomes arising from student, faculty, and staff engagement with community, shifting from service-learning as a pedagogical tool toward a focus on civic learning outcomes (Saltmarsh, 2005). With social entrepreneurship, the paradigmatic shift attempts to decenter the entrepreneur's perceived benefits, shifting the value proposition toward a private and social value equilibrium. With a new focus on civic outcomes and community benefit, institutions began the process to identify how to evaluate engagement, what to evaluate, and who should be included as the intended beneficiaries of engagement. Ultimately, the focus arising from the first paradigmatic shift resulted in an integration between service and academic study in the public good–based trajectory, with an emphasis on a reflective, community-based pedagogy (Saltmarsh, 2005). Similarly, for the market-based trajectory, the first paradigmatic shift emphasizes movement away from the entrepreneur toward societal benefit (Martin & Osberg, 2007).

The public good–based trajectory of engagement took the nascent origins of community service, where students volunteered their time to local communities, and developed a service-learning frame to help students gain a more holistic and impactful experience (Finley, 2011). Institutions were promoting student participation in their communities without intentional or politically oriented purpose. In this dynamic, students and other college or university members were extracting benefit from service without any formal accountability structure to protect community partners from exploitation. While this form of participation persisted throughout the 1990s, scholars and practitioners began critically evaluating their participation with community partners, citing heterogeneity in practice. As the American Association of State Colleges and Universities (AASCU) noted in a 2002 report, publicly oriented service-learning engagement served as

> shorthand for describing a new era of two-way partnerships between America's colleges and universities and the publics they serve. . . . [I]t also presents the risk that the term can say everything and nothing at the same time. . . . [T]he lack of clear definition can leave some campuses and their leaders with the impression that they are "doing engagement," when in fact they are not. (p. 8)

The AASCU's report highlighted college and university engagement with community partners that lacked explicit intentions and accountability structures.

In response to the shortcomings of partnerships between community members and postsecondary institutions, institutions began to think about the civic nature of their engagement. Some institutions may have perceived their community partnership as a form of civic engagement, though these types of partnerships were apolitical or divorced from civic processes or aims (Finley, 2011). As criticisms grew regarding campus partnerships, institutions shifted their focus toward the students' learning outcomes because existing partnerships were "not sufficiently or substantially connected to a student's role within a larger community or processes of negotiation (i.e. dialogue and deliberation)," and "apolitical experiences encourage students to focus reflection inward on their individual experience, rather than outward to the relevance of that experience to a societal big picture" (Finley, 2011, p. 4). To intentionally incorporate civic goals and outcomes as part of student engagement with the local community, scholars advocated for training students in the skills of democracy (Colby, Beaumont, Ehrlich, & Corngold, 2007; Colby, Ehrlich, Beaumont, & Stephens, 2003; Finley, 2011; Scobey, 2010; Thomas, 2011). This shift, embodied in what we refer to as the first paradigm, resulted in institutions moving toward civic engagement as a framework for practice, away from service-learning. Civic engagement is more attentive to impact and reciprocity within community partnerships, because it is no longer "an isolated, unreflective, or unintentional experience" (Finley, 2011, p. 13).

A parallel, but distinct, market-based trajectory of engagement emerged in tandem with service-learning. Grounded primarily in business programs, the concept of social entrepreneurship emerged from the entrepreneurship research applied to student engagement, which values applying business strategies to solve social issues (Dees, 2001; McBride & Mlyn, 2016). Dees (2001) offers a multifaceted definition for *social entrepreneurship*: Entrepreneurs enter the social sector in order to create and sustain social value; pursue new opportunities; engage in consistent innovation, adaptation, and learning; and embrace the possibility of risk while remaining accountable to the constituencies served. Building on Dee's foundational definition, Martin and Osberg (2007) broadly view entrepreneurship as an opportunity for transformational benefit that emerges in an "unjust equilibrium that causes the exclusion, marginalization, or suffering of a segment of humanity that lacks the financial means or political clout to achieve any transformative benefit on its own" (para. 40). Improving on the earlier definitions of *social entrepreneurship*, the distinction between social and nonsocial entrepreneurship now lies in the value proposition of the social entrepreneur no longer anticipating significant financial capital. Rather, "the social entrepreneur aims for value in the form of large-scale, transformational benefit that accrues either to a significant segment of society or to society at large" (Martin & Osberg, 2007, para. 39). The goal of social entrepreneurship is to create something new that meets a social need. Yet, social entrepreneurship still remains focused on private gain, to distinguish itself as entrepreneurship, rather than philanthropy. Even after social entrepreneurship developed into social innovation, the tension between social and private value still persists.

Importantly, the constituencies that are served remain heterogeneous, and the value propositions in social entrepreneurship still privilege the entrepreneur, especially as they pertain to student engagement. For example, social entrepreneurship can mean a student partnering with a not-for-profit organization to start a for-profit venture or any individual student starting a not-for-profit organization (Dees, 2001). The beneficiaries, in these cases, are the entrepreneur, the student, or the shareholders, not necessarily any communities that colleges or universities partner with in the name of social entrepreneurship. Furthermore, even if engagement was centered on providing solutions to social problems, social entrepreneurship did not fully incorporate the local communities' perspectives on setting the agenda for social change.

The last two decades have seen a growth in the level of business engagement with the governmental and nonprofit sectors, such that there has been a "proliferation of terms that juxtapose the word 'social' with private sector concepts, producing such new terms as *social entrepreneurship*, *social enterprise*, and . . . *social innovation*" (Phills, Deiglmeier, & Miller, 2008, para. 2, emphasis added). In this neoliberal appropriation of "the social," scholars have critiqued social entrepreneurship's problematic tendency to harbor "a kind of end-orientation and conservatism which neutralises the concept's radically transformative possibilities" (Dey & Steyaert, 2012, p. 91). Further, scholars problematize the emphasis on entrepreneurship as a theory of change, which assumes entrepreneurship is "always stimulating and worthwhile to pursue, as something that does not require any reflection" (Dey & Steyaert, 2012, p. 92; see also Armstrong, 2005; Jones & Spicer, 2009; Ogbor, 2000; and Weiskopf & Steyaert, 2009). Similar to the critiques of service-learning, critical research critiqued social entrepreneurship's engagement as one sided, where the student or the entrepreneur was the intended beneficiary.

These critiques represented the first paradigmatic shift occurring in the market-based trajectory of student engagement. As a response to these critiques, social innovation emerged as an alternative framing for student engagement that shifted focus away from the entrepreneur and toward the community. For example, Martin and Osberg (2007) make a distinction between social entrepreneurship, on one hand, and social service and social activism, on the other. A fundamental aspect of both social service and social activism that makes them distinct from social entrepreneurship is that the entrepreneur is not centralized. Unlike social entrepreneurship, social service and social activism lack the ability and foresight to scale their efforts; if they could scale their efforts, then the endeavors would be more in line with social entrepreneurship. Scale is important because it signifies the existence of a vision, and the presence of a vision "anchors [one's] reputation as a social entrepreneur" (Martin & Osberg, 2007, para. 54). In the lack of attention to context and intended beneficiaries of social entrepreneurship, social innovation emerged as a more capacious concept that included processes, technologies, social movements, or ideas intimately tied to ameliorating a social problem (Phills et al., 2008). In contrast to social entrepreneurship, social innovation shifts the focus from the entrepreneur to the process, emphasizing innovation across departments, disciplines, and communities. Although scale can be important for achieving *more* results in social innovation, that is not a primary concern for social innovation because the entrepreneur's reputation is not constitutive of social innovation.

The first paradigmatic shift marks a change in how colleges and universities engage with their community. Progressing from thinking of students as the intended beneficiary or sole actor in engagement, civic engagement and social innovation are more thoughtful about the two-sided, reciprocal nature of their engagement.

Paradigm Two's Effect on Trajectories

The second paradigmatic shift, which we call power relations and shared context, identifies the limitations in the public good–based and market-based trajectories' existing practices with their communities. With civic engagement, the paradigmatic shift results in reflective practices emphasizing how power and shared context operate among students, colleges and universities, and the communities with which they engage. Scholarly research, most notably an article by Saltmarsh, Hartley, and Clayton (2009), urges institutions to consider their engagement as part of a deliberative and democratic society where college and university members' work is part of building a democratic society. In social innovation, practitioners and scholars attempt to move beyond the boundaries and limitations imposed by social entrepreneurship—where the entrepreneur's goals were primary—toward redefining innovation and societal impact. Unlike civic engagement, social innovation has not systematically responded to calls for reflexive engagement with their communities. In this section, we review how the public good–based trajectory attends to power relations and shared context to produce democratic civic engagement and map a path toward democratic social innovation.

Along the public good–based trajectory, civic engagement focuses on outcomes resulting from student engagement with the local community. As a result, civic engagement takes the infrastructure of service-learning and focuses on depth, rather than breadth, of engagement. Institutions of higher education accomplish this by integrating civic engagement into the core functions of the university: the generation and dissemination of knowledge (Saltmarsh, 2005). Responding to earlier critiques that service-learning lacked clarity and coherence, the literature on civic engagement advocates for a cohesive definition and establishing "a set of skills essential for democracy-building and [viewing civic engagement] as an activity that is fundamentally politically-oriented" (Finley, 2011, p. 20). By integrating civic renewal into the institutional agenda, civic engagement "gained widespread acceptance as the encompassing conceptual framework" (Saltmarsh, 2005, p. 52).

Civic engagement was a marked improvement from service-learning because of its intentional approach to student engagement. Although civic engagement was successful in creating the metrics and the discourse to monitor and evaluate the institutionalization of impact and reciprocity on campuses, it fell short of its democratic goal in practice. College and university members were more conscientious in their engagement with the community but were not fully considering the community's role in defining the agenda. For example, to limit the negative consequences of students coming and going annually in their engagement, colleges and universities worked to establish long-lasting relationships between campus and community partners. Yet this focus on students' outcomes and impact did not recognize the power dynamics and shared context between the campus and community partners. Namely, community partners were not necessarily able to define areas of need or have a role in recruiting partners from the campus; community partnerships in this dynamic continued to center and privilege the needs of campus members over community members.

More recently, a push emerged to further reframe this work as democratic civic engagement, because practitioners recognized that the institution focused on students' presence in the community but was not reflecting on its own presence in the communities in which it engaged. Democratic civic engagement offers a way for colleges and universities to play a more active role in responding to societal challenges by more explicitly defining its goals, efforts, and ideologies of practice (Saltmarsh et al., 2009). Because "an educational ethos of unencumbered individualism has a very high cost in the neglect and diminishment of democratic society" (Knefelkamp & Schneider, 1997, p. 333), democratic civic engagement as a framework prompted institutions to think holistically about the full engagement experience as a true partnership in a democratic society.

Saltmarsh and colleagues (2009) argue for the adoption of democratic civic engagement as an avenue for higher education to respond to societal challenges. Traditional approaches to civic engagement faltered as a result of unclear goals, fragmented efforts, and predominant ideologies in the academy that are contrary to the principles of impact, reciprocity, power relations, and shared context. Democratic civic engagement means that "democratic values are part of the leadership of administrators, the scholarly work of faculty, the educational work of staff, and the leadership development and learning outcomes of students" (Saltmarsh et al., 2009 p. 6). As such, democratic civic engagement, Saltmarsh and colleagues argue, has epistemological, curricular, pedagogical, research, policy, and culture implications for transforming higher education.This framework for civic engagement was more attuned toward power relations because the goal was to identify whether knowledge produced in the academy and its use were inclusive of other types of knowledge and approaches to problem-solving (Saltmarsh et al., 2009).

The inclusion of democratic principles fundamentally centers student engagement within the community, rather than solely on the individual. To build on efforts of reflexivity in student engagement, democratic civic engagement also serves as a unifying framework for diversity and inclusion initiatives. With a focus on power relations, including diversity and inclusion efforts as part of democratic civic engagement means that student engagement is now also aimed at altering systemic obstacles and injustices in higher education. The challenge in integrating democratic civic engagement and diversity and inclusion comes in the form of whether the approach to change was thick or thin. In other words, a thick approach to integration means systemically connecting "student success with faculty diversity, faculty diversity with community engagement and inclusive pedagogical practices, faculty diversity with engaged scholarship, and engaged scholarship with institutional rewards and supportive institutional cultures" (Sturm, Eatman, Saltmarsh, & Bush, 2011, p. 12). The approach takes seriously the various stakeholders within higher education and what role they should play in transforming higher education along democratic principles, as a response to the second paradigmatic shift.

In a similar way, along the market-based trajectory of student engagement, social innovation is attempting to reconcile its tensions with social entrepreneurship. Social innovation poses a "novel solution to a social problem that is more effective, efficient, sustainable, or just than existing solutions and for which the value created accrues primarily to society as a whole rather than private individuals" (Phills et al., 2008, para. 3). Rather than describing the sectors or sources of financial capital as representative of how innovation is social, the definition views social innovation as a process, a technology, a movement, or an idea intimately tied to ameliorating a social problem. For example, under this definition, a piece of legislation and a social movement could both be considered social innovations because the primary benefits are societal. As we have learned from earlier articulations of socially oriented private enterprises, social innovation in this vein "transcends sectors, levels of analysis, and methods to discover the processes—the strategies, tactics, and theories of change—that produce lasting impact" (Phills et al., 2008, para. 11).

Unlike social entrepreneurship, a single entity or a single entrepreneur does not embody social innovation. As discussed earlier, social innovation considers what a social need is as part of what makes it social innovation, setting it apart from social entrepreneurship in how it values the community versus the entrepreneur (Phills et al., 2008). Under social entrepreneurship, consideration of the social good would count as social services or social activism (Martin & Osberg, 2007), yet social innovation now views those causes and the community they impact within its definition, not outside it. Freed from the narrow definition of *entrepreneurship* in the business and finance departments, social innovation can occur at many levels, including the organization, and in many different disciplines or fields. While social entrepreneurship is often focused on the creation of something new that entrepreneurs can use to build their status, social innovation can be an improvement or investment into existing structures and operation. With less of a focus on reinventing the wheel, in some senses, social innovation can become a collective endeavor for the progress of society, because the work is centered on the social problem and not on the ingenuity of the entrepreneur. Yet, similar to the shortcomings in social entrepreneurship's past practices being centered on the entrepreneur's—or the college's or university's—solutions and knowledge, social innovation does not incorporate community-based knowledge into its practices (Sharma, 2016). While social innovation is positioned as significantly different from social entrepreneurship, in practice, the "social" serves as a description in which colleges and universities are seeing and acting on opportunities for value creation. Social innovation's motivating spirit to rectify the imbalance between private and social value generation, which separates it from social entrepreneurship, has not been fully realized.

Democratic social innovation provides a framework through which social innovation could realize its animating spirit and further differentiate itself from social entrepreneurship. Through a greater attention to structural and historical processes, democratic social innovation aims to decenter the epistemological core of the entrepreneur, innovator, or expert and centers the community in the coproduction of social change. Similar to civic engagement, social innovation does not consider the community's role in defining the social problem, the scope of solutions, or the methods for achieving success (Sharma, 2017). Democratic social innovation addresses this neocolonial tension through a deliberative approach with community partners to center the community's experiences and needs and leverage college and university resources to that end. The shift in democratic social innovation is one in which power moves from being solely vested in the college and university toward a shared ownership with the community.

Similarly, as civic engagement lacks an explicit focus on diversity and inclusion efforts ongoing in higher education, social innovation approaches attempt to solve social problems without addressing underlying structural issues. Democratic social innovation is attuned to diversity and inclusion efforts and broadens who is considered an agent and the intention motivating collaborations between the campus and community. A focus on diversity and inclusion as an integral component of democratic social innovation means that partnerships are community defined. The integration of efforts enacted under democratic social innovation forces the institution to reflect on its own historical power dynamics with the community over time.

Democratic social innovation has an intentional focus on outcomes for the community, defined by the community. In contrast, social entrepreneurship's and social innovation's outcomes are beholden to different stakeholders: the investor, the customer, the donor, the college or university. For example, the focus on the beneficiaries can be seen in how donors engage with university coursework. Through investments in social entrepreneurship and social innovation courses, these enriched universities can "legitimately add to their community welfare credentials and churn out graduates who aim to be job-creators and not just job-seekers, [making] the pull of social entrepreneurship [and social innovation] too strong to resist for many schools" (Sharma, 2016, para. 14). These ongoing power dynamics, in which donors are more actively engaging with colleges and universities, require a framework through which to manage these external investors. Lacking such a framework opens up college and university classrooms to the highest bidder, contributing to the neoliberalization of higher education (Berman, 2012; Slaughter & Rhoades, 2000). In addition, some campuses charge community partners for social innovation internships. As a result, "the partner not only pays the student for [their] time, but also pays the higher education institution for assigning the student" (McBride & Mlyn, 2016, para. 11). Conceptualizing community partners as investors or clients shifts the focus toward profit, rather than addressing social change.

Democratic social innovation provides a framework that not only challenges neoliberal processes but also helps institutions avoid the trap of creating crises simply for the sake of solving them (Jones & Murtola, 2012). Because democratic social innovation dislocates the power from colleges and universities and empowers community partners, the framework provides the pathway for a form of wealth transfer from the elite. In current social innovation approaches, philanthropic investments from the wealthy support the same systems that codified their wealth. Democratic social innovation disrupts this cyclical wealth transfer by enabling the community partners to set the agenda and truly centering the community partners' needs and benefits.

The second paradigmatic shift represents a reimagination of how student engagement is connected to assumptions about expertise, attends to efforts on diversity and inclusion, and redefines the relationship with community partners. By attending to power relations and shared context, democratic civic engagement and democratic social innovation have the potential to alter how higher education functions in a democracy.

In the next section, we turn to empirical analyses of the ongoing movement from social entrepreneurship to social innovation. The findings suggest that a feasible pathway to operationalize democratic social innovation exists, through institutional guidance for programmatic self-assessment on the issues of power and shared context. With institutional guidance social innovation can respond to the second paradigmatic shift, focused on power relations and shared context.

Data and Findings

To explore how these theoretical issues manifest in higher education programming, we focus on the following empirical research questions: (a) How do institutions of higher education engage with social innovation and social entrepreneurship through academic programming? (b) Are *social entrepreneurship* and *social innovation* defined as distinct concepts? (c) To what extent do campuses combine social entrepreneurship, social innovation, and civic engagement, or are conceptualizations distinct? To address these questions, we leveraged publicly available data on social entrepreneurship and innovation among Ashoka U higher education institutions ($n = 44$). In addition, we surveyed campuses to identify existing linkages among social entrepreneurship, innovation, and community engagement ($n = 13$). Ashoka U is an initiative to connect campuses investing in social entrepreneurship; the organization views any individual as a potential changemaker and it aims to help institutions of higher education "break down barriers to institutional change and foster a campus-wide culture of social innovation" (Ashoka U, 2018, para. 1). We use the Ashoka U network to identify campuses that have a stated commitment to social entrepreneurship and social innovation because this group is more likely to have public language demonstrating engagement with social innovation, social entrepreneurship, and civic engagement through academic programming. In sampling these campuses, we provide a conservative estimate of how well these three concepts may be integrated at institutions of higher education that are investing in them.

We collected data from public courses during the 2016–2017 academic year that listed social entrepreneurship or social innovation in their course title or description. We noted the department offering the course, the number of courses offered under these titles, and any potential cross listings. Interestingly, there were few cross-listed courses; we chose to list them separately as part of both social entrepreneurship and social innovation totals. We also explored websites of Ashoka U campuses with centers for social innovation and social entrepreneurship to identify any definitions, missions, and statements of purpose.

Finally, we conducted a survey focusing on campuses' curricular programming and their process of defining social innovation and social entrepreneurship and how the definitions relate to Carnegie's definition of community engagement. The brief survey was sent to a cohort with a range of student population sizes, geographies, and educational foci that were engaged with innovation and community engagement work. In collaboration with colleagues at Ashoka U and the Bonner Foundation, we generated a list of 26 campuses. We created 2 high-yield questions to test, the first asking the institution how it defines *social innovation*, how it reached that definition, and how that definition compares to the Carnegie definition of *community engagement*; and the second asking the institution to summarize its curricular and cocurricular offerings in social innovation. Of the 26 surveyed campuses, 13 campuses responded.

The data collection efforts focused on the following goals: First, we identify existing institutional architecture through course listings within and across departments. These data measure interdisciplinary collaborative academic efforts. Second, through collecting definitions and missions of social entrepreneurship and innovation, we trace the theoretical bridges and gaps between social entrepreneurship and social innovation. Third, the survey prompts institutions of higher education to think about potential synergies among social entrepreneurship, social innovation, and community engagement.

Table 7.1 summarizes the findings from the course list search. The departments were categorized along three broad dimensions of business, management, and economics; social sciences and humanities; and entrepreneurship and innovation. When we looked at one academic year, it became evident that there was hypersegmentation by not only departments across campuses but also types of courses departments offered. Hypersegmentation in this sense means that there were few cross-listed or overlapping courses. For example, we found that across departments, business, management, and economics offered marginally more total courses in social entrepreneurship and social innovation compared to the other two departments, but in aggregate, there was no preference between social entrepreneurship and social innovation, with 72 and 70 courses offered in each, respectively. Entrepreneurship and innovation departments offered the fewest overall courses. Given that the latter types of departments are not often separated from business and management schools, the lower number of courses is not surprising.

TABLE 7.1
Number of Identifiable Courses Offered at Ashoka U Institutions in Academic Year 2016–2017

Department	*Social Entrepreneurship*	*Social Innovation*	*Total Courses Offered*
Business, management, and economics	24	31	55
Social sciences and humanities	28	22	50
Entrepreneurship and innovation	18	19	37
Total	70	72	142

When disaggregating within these departmental dimensions, marginally more courses in social innovation were offered in business, management, and economics departments, while marginally more courses in social entrepreneurship were offered in social sciences and humanities departments. A substantive number of institutions offered departmental focuses on entrepreneurship and innovation, and we found that these departments offered about the same amount of courses in social entrepreneurship and social innovation. Although we studied only one academic year, we found that many of these courses were offered regularly in past years. Table 7.1 suggests that there was a disparity in total course offerings for social entrepreneurship and social innovation *across departments* at institutions committed to *both* these topics and that, within departments, business, management, and economics departments had a slight lean toward social innovation while social sciences and humanities offered more social entrepreneurship courses. Departments of entrepreneurship and innovation had relative parity in course offerings for social entrepreneurship and social innovation.

These findings suggest that as institutions are responding to the first paradigm of impact and reciprocity in student engagement, to the extent that coursework is part of that response, disciplinary variation must be considered. For example, while business, management, and economics departments are colloquially considered the center of social entrepreneurship work, our data indicate that these departments may be moving toward social innovation as the next frontier. In contrast, social sciences and humanities departments are making a shift toward social entrepreneurship because they may have historically been focused on the public good trajectory and civic engagement. While departments provide a course offering in social entrepreneurship and social innovation, Table 7.1 provides evidence that the paradigmatic shift we identify as impact and reciprocity is playing out in business, management, and economics departments, while social sciences and humanities departments are following that pathway at a different pace. Given that the challenges presented in paradigm two are partially the result of ineffective institutional responses to the challenges presented in paradigm one, the disciplinary variation observed here is not entirely surprising. We argue that it provides opportunity for synergy across departments because the trajectories are forward moving and cumulative.

Table 7.2 summarizes the data collected on campus definitions of *social innovation* and *social entrepreneurship*. It presents keywords by linguistic themes, focusing on market-based concepts, common good and social justice, problem orientation and identification, and relational language. There are three key takeaways from this analysis:

1. Market-based language is the most prevalent category, and higher education programs, centers, and departments rely heavily on this type of language to communicate commitments to social entrepreneurship, in particular.
2. The common good and problem orientation categories are very similar across institutional definitions; colleges and universities are relying on similar problem identification language in definitions of *social entrepreneurship* and *social innovation.*
3. The definitions do not use relational language to communicate the importance of reciprocity and mutuality in social entrepreneurship and innovation.

The preliminary evidence suggests that higher education institutions are defining *social entrepreneurship* and *social innovation* as something that is done *to* rather than *with* the community. This suggests that social innovation and social entrepreneurship continue to grapple with the paradigmatic emphasis on reciprocity and have yet to address the second paradigm's emphasis on power relations and shared context.

The informal survey of 13 higher education institutions posed the following substantive questions on social entrepreneurship and social innovation:

- What curricular and/or cocurricular programming does your institution have to support students interested in learning the skills and processes for creating innovative solutions to social problems?

- Please tell us how your institution defines *social innovation,* and how you came to that definition. How does that definition compare to Carnegie's following definition of *community engagement:* the collaboration between institutions of higher education and their larger communities (local, regional/state, national, global) for the mutually beneficial exchange of knowledge and resources in a context of partnership and reciprocity?

TABLE 7.2
Keywords in Definitions at Ashoka U Institutions in Academic Year 2016–2017

	Social Innovation	*Social Entrepreneurship*
Market-based language	Business, economic, outcomes, entrepreneurial, innovative, efficient, scalable, viable, prosperity, measurable, self-sustaining	Resources, enterprise, business management mind-set, competition, supply chain, design thinking, measurable, revenue driven, financial sustainability, scale, business models, competition, experiment, ambitious, start-up, philanthropy, market-based solutions, responsible management, mobilizing resources, systems change, venture
Common good–social justice language	Common good outcomes, just, mission-driven, capacity, social value	Common good, social value, opportunities, social venture, social responsibility, social mission
Problem orientation–identification language	Intervention, social problem, societal dilemmas, critical social problems, persistent social problems, systemic, local, global	Marginalized groups, innovative solutions, social ills, social problems, intractable social need
Relational language	Relationships, ecosystem, leaders, environmental, awareness, sustainable, community, collaborate	Interdisciplinary, community networks, environmental

The first question focuses on curricular programming intended to support students in creating innovative solutions to social problems. We summarize the institutions' responses and do not provide identifying information for privacy concerns; if any institutional affiliations were redacted, these institutions would still be identifiable given the nature of the information they provide and the small sample size. Respondents highlight synergies across departments and note opportunities to engage in interdisciplinary collaboration through internships, community service, service-learning, and funding prizes for student ventures. All dually recognized Ashoka U and Carnegie campuses had undergraduate and graduate courses related to social innovation and social entrepreneurship. Each institution had a different way of supporting students interested in social innovation, including incubators, grant funding for engaged work, competitions, residential communities, and offices. Carnegie-classified respondents had far fewer curricular offerings; several offer cocurricular programming. Bonner campuses have the fewest programs, with their resources being more related to community engagement than social innovation.

The second question asks institutions to define *social innovation*, identify the source of the definition, and compare it to the Carnegie definition of *community engagement*. From the data collected, we found that organizations that had both Ashoka U and Carnegie accreditation had the most comprehensive philosophy and pedagogy related to *social innovation*. Organizations that were only Carnegie classified had far fewer campus offerings related to social innovation, and many had no definition for *social innovation*. Four institutions had no definition of *social innovation*; one provided a definition of *social entrepreneurship*. All Ashoka U campuses provided a definition of *social innovation*; only one Bonner campus provided a definition: "projects/programs that are aimed at enhancing the public good." We would argue that this is not an adequate representation of social innovation. This indicates that, although many campuses are working in what they consider to be social innovation, the nascent field does not have clarity in a shared definition.

Of the organizations we surveyed, most viewed social entrepreneurship, social innovation, and civic engagement as disparate commitments, not part of a cohesive program for social change. Of the 13 respondents, 6 offered definitions of *social innovation* with no explicit connection to community engagement. The definitions of *social innovation* were about students creating processes of change, and many of these institutions simply provided a definition that was indistinguishable from that of social entrepreneurship. Three additional campuses defined *social innovation* as focused on "outcomes" or "solutions" and civic engagement as a method of partnership, "collaboration," or "strateg[y] or proce[ss]." Three other institutions offered no institutional definition of *social innovation*. Lastly, 1 respondent encouraged students to work with community partners in order to develop students' leadership potential and growth. In reviewing these perspectives, we concluded that partnerships with the community were seen as a tool for student development, extracting resources and knowledge from the community, rather than as reciprocal partnerships. While some institutions provided no definition for *social innovation*, those that did define *social entrepreneurship*, *social innovation*, and *community engagement* discussed engagement as a tool for students, not as a way to strengthen ties with community partners. These institutions' definitions for these terms revealed that the focus remained on student benefit. Another institution echoed this precise sentiment, suggesting collaboration with social innovators as a pedagogical tool to supplement coursework in social innovation. This provides further evidence that colleges and universities are still struggling to implement the norms of mutual and reciprocal relationships with community members when they practice social entrepreneurship, social innovation, and community engagement.

Discussion

The theoretical framings and findings demonstrate the tensions in theory and in practice in social innovation. With the public good–based trajectory, we describe the epistemological progress in defining, implementing, and measuring democratic civic engagement in higher education. Next, we draw on theoretical insights from scholars and practitioners to consider how impact, reciprocity, power relations, and shared context affected this process. We applied these theoretical paradigms of democratic civic engagement to the market-based trajectory for engagement, proposing a shift toward democratic social innovation. In response to our research questions, we highlight disciplinary fragmentation in course offerings and heterogeneity in institutional definitions for *social innovation* and *social entrepreneurship*. As Table 7.2 and the survey responses reveal, higher education institutions are conceptualizing social entrepreneurship and innovation as something that is *done to* rather than *with* the community. Institutions engaging in social innovation and social entrepreneurship continue to grapple with the paradigmatic emphasis on reciprocity and still have not addressed the second paradigm's emphasis on power relations and shared context. In an effort to institutionalize democratic civic engagement as a process, colleges and universities have adopted the

Carnegie classification to track, measure, and hold themselves accountable to the principles of power relations and shared context. The findings suggest that a similar approach for social innovation and social entrepreneurship programs could usher in a theoretically grounded praxis for implementing democratic social innovation.

The Carnegie Foundation for the Advancement of Teaching piloted a "classification for community engagement" (Saltmarsh & Hartley, 2011, p. 3) in 2005, as part of a broader effort to clarify and unify efforts toward community engagement on campus. The Carnegie classification has three major dimensions of focus: foundational indicators, such as institutional commitment and institutional identity and culture, curricular engagement, and outreach and partnerships. The classification is not a ranking tool and respects the diversity among institutions and how they approach community engagement; the classification encourages a process of inquiry, reflection, and self-assessment (Driscoll, 2008). In this way, the classification highlights the

> partnership of college and university knowledge and resources with those of the public and private sectors to enrich scholarship, research, and creative activity; enhance curriculum, teaching and learning; prepare educated, engaged citizens; strengthen democratic values and civic responsibility; address critical societal issues; and contribute to the public good. (Saltmarsh & Johnson, 2018, p. 4)

The classification provides a lens to evaluate the reciprocity, the potential exploitation, and the mutuality of relationships that colleges and universities form with their students, staff, faculty, and greater community. Ultimately, the classification incentivizes genuine collaboration: "Learning and teaching [are] multidirectional and the expertise [is] shared. It represents a basic reconceptualization of . . . community-based work" (O'Meara & Rice, 2005, p. 11).

Engaging with the Carnegie classification encourages institutions to think about the depth and breadth of their commitments to the principles of power relations and shared context through social innovation and civic engagement. It also encourages colleges and universities to evaluate their institutional infrastructure as it relates to how funding is allocated across campus, how community-engaged scholarship is valued in promotion and tenure requirements for faculty, how many courses are offered across different departments, and how many students across campus take part in this coursework. While the classification is not prescriptive, organizing campus efforts through the framework counteracts potential departmental fragmentation by focusing on institutional cohesion and highlighting areas of synergy.

The data analysis reveals the potential redundancies and missed opportunities for collaboration. For example, Table 7.1 suggests that departments are moving in different directions in terms of the focuses of their course offerings for social entrepreneurship and social innovation. Similarly, the analyses on definitions of *social entrepreneurship* and *social innovation* highlight a divergence of how centers devoted to social entrepreneurship and social innovation are focusing their efforts. The survey results highlight the in-class and extracurricular avenues for participating in social innovation and learning, but how these opportunities are communicated across disparate departments to interested students and faculty remains unclear. Whether this divergence is productive or redundant requires more empirical research and systematic study, but the Carnegie classification provides a framework for identifying structural pathways for collaborations.

The Carnegie classification encourages institutions to think systematically about their response to the second paradigmatic shift, cultivating partnerships with community members that are attuned to potential power imbalances between the community and institutions of higher education. This is a critical area for growth identified in our preliminary data analysis: Courses, definitions, and survey responses appear disconnected from meaningful community partnership and collaboration. It is imperative that social innovation be conceived as a partnership *with* the community, rather than *for* the community. Although we cannot evaluate the substance of existing relationships across and beyond campuses, the preliminary data analyses call for scholars to empirically identify whether existing campus structural relations truly engage with the community, or whether these partnerships fail to match Carnegie's articulation of community partnerships. Carnegie does not guarantee the ideal outcomes, but it does provide an architecture and approach for benchmarking and tracking progress toward symbiotic relationships with the community.

In shifting the focus to include community partnerships, Carnegie articulates student engagement for a social good through democratic civic engagement and democratic social innovation. For example, the classification emphasizes that relationships between on- and off-campus organizations

> are grounded in the qualities of reciprocity, mutual respect, shared authority, and co-creation of goals and outcomes. Such relationships are

> by their very nature trans-disciplinary (knowledge transcending the disciplines and the college or university) and asset-based (where the strengths, skills, and knowledge of those in the community are validated and legitimized). (Saltmarsh & Johnson, 2018, p. 5)

In the context of democratic civic engagement and democratic social innovation, the classification encourages institutions to value community-based knowledge and experience.

As a result, the classification is more explicitly tied to ongoing diversity and inclusion initiatives because these initiatives consider the position colleges and universities occupy in society and the potential social benefits that could accrue if institutions were more committed to justice. By connecting diversity and inclusion with civic engagement through the Carnegie classification, it is possible to connect "the knowledge resources of the academy with the pressing and complex problems facing multiple communities" and build "the capacity and commitment of diverse leadership equipped to tackle these social problems" (Sturm et al., 2011, p. 7). These priorities are relevant for social innovation on college and university campuses because of their commitment to ameliorating social problems and developing impactful leadership for a changing world. In attuning the Carnegie classification—a framework for shifting civic engagement and social entrepreneurship to democratic civic engagement and democratic social innovation, respectively—to diversity and inclusion, we arrive at a holistic approach for college and university engagement with local and global communities. The approach attends to the critiques that initially prompted the two paradigm shifts in engagement in higher education by operationalizing the democratic civic engagement and democratic social innovation approaches.

For example, in following those approaches, partnerships center marginalized voices to build reciprocity and embed reflexivity into the partnership, recognize power relations pervaded within partnerships, and mitigate the exploitation of the shared economic and political contexts. The classification provides a tool to aid colleges and universities in this process because it not only encourages applicants to reflect on what diversity and inclusion looks like on their own campuses and given their own histories but also provides a pathway for meeting these challenges. In doing this, the classification does not impose a singular vision of engagement attentive to diversity and inclusion onto all campuses.

Social entrepreneurship and social innovation are growing on college and university campuses in the United States and across the globe as institutions are investing more in civic engagement. While some call for bridging a gap between social innovation and civic engagement, we argue that there are two distinct trajectories in student engagement efforts. The public good–based trajectory has attended to the principles of impact, reciprocity, power relations, and shared context and arrived at democratic civic engagement as the current form of practice. Through the Carnegie classification, democratic civic engagement prompts institutions to reconsider the core dynamics of their community partnerships and institutional commitments. In providing a framework for benchmarking and measuring process relating to community engagement and diversity and inclusion, the classification aids institutions in identifying areas of strengths and further growth.

Along a second trajectory of market-based student engagement, practitioners and scholars have argued that social innovation is a socially conscious framework for engaging in community partnerships. The logic for this argument is that universities are problem-solvers, not coproducers with community partners. As we have argued, though, social innovation may respond to concerns of impact and reciprocity but has yet to meet the transformative challenge that power relations and shared context offer. As our analyses highlight, institutions are defining *social innovation* by outcomes that are centered on student growth, with limited attention to how engagement is helping the community partner. The challenge of power relations and shared context demands an epistemological decentering of the university and innovators to recognize and create avenues for collaborative knowledge generation with the community. Without meeting this challenge, social innovation may lose its distinction from social entrepreneurship because the community partners remain guests at the table, rather than key decision-makers. Amending Scobey's (2015) call to bridge the divide between social innovation and civic engagement, we argue for using the Carnegie classification to promote democratic civic engagement and democratic social innovation. The process of classification aids institutions in reevaluating their practices and structures on campus to push civic engagement and social innovation toward democratic sensibilities. The classification itself is a starting point, though. As the Carnegie reclassification process indicates, the classification intends for institutions to continually engage in evaluation, remaining open to increasingly higher expectations for community engagement and social innovation. While an external review process, such as the classification, is productive to this end, we also argue that institutions engage in internal, reflective evaluation to ensure that the standards of evaluation are appropriate for their institution and their community partners. If truly transformative work is to occur on college and university campuses for the social good, then any architecture for engagement must focus on interdisciplinary collaboration and reciprocal community partnerships. The Carnegie classification provides one such frame.

References

American Association of State Colleges and Universities. (2002). *Stepping forward as stewards of place.* Washington, DC: Author.

Armstrong, P. (2005). *Critique of entrepreneurship: People and policy.* London, UK: Palgrave Macmillan.

Ashoka U. (2018). *About Ashoka U.* Retrieved from https://www.ashoka.org/en-US/program/ashoka-u

Berman, E. P. (2012). *Creating the market university: How academic science became an economic engine.* Princeton, NJ: Princeton University Press.

Colby, A., Beaumont, E., Ehrlich, T., & Corngold, J. (2007). *Educating for democracy: Preparing undergraduates for responsible political engagement.* San Francisco, CA: Jossey-Bass.

Colby, A., Ehrlich, T., Beaumont, E., & Stephens, J. (2003). *Educating citizens: Preparing America's undergraduates for lives of moral and civic responsibility.* San Francisco, CA: Jossey-Bass.

Dees, J. G. (2001). *The meaning of "social entrepreneurship,* 1–5. Kansas City, MO and Palo Alto, CA: Kauffman Foundation and Stanford University.

Dey, P., & Steyaert, C. (2012). Social entrepreneurship: Critique and the radical enactment of the social. *Social Enterprise Journal, 8*(2), 90–107.

Driscoll, A. (2008). Carnegie's community-engagement classification: Intentions and insights. *Change: The Magazine of Higher Learning, 40*(1), 38–41.

Drucker, P. F. (1985). *Innovation and entrepreneurship: Practice and principles.* New York, NY: Harper Business.

Finley, A. (2011, May 24). *Civic learning and democratic engagements: A review of the literature on civic engagement in post-secondary education.* Paper prepared for the U.S. Department of Education, Association of American Colleges & Universities, Washington, DC.

Jones, C., & Murtola, A.-M. (2012). Entrepreneurship, crisis, critique. In D. Hjorth (Ed.), *Handbook on organisational entrepreneurship* (pp. 116–133). Cheltenham, UK: Edward Elgar.

Jones, C., & Spicer, A. (2009). *Unmasking the entrepreneur.* Cheltenham, UK: Edward Elgar.

Knefelkamp, L., & Schneider, C. (1997). Education for a world lived in common with others. In R. Orrill (Ed.), *Education and democracy: Re-imagining liberal learning in America* (pp. 327–344). New York, NY: College Entrance Examination Board.

Martin, R. L., & Osberg, S. (2007, Spring). Social entrepreneurship: The case for definition. *Stanford Social Innovation Review.* Retrieved from https://ssir.org/articles/entry/social_entrepreneurship_the_case_for_definition

McBride, A., & Mlyn, E. (2016). Social innovation and civic engagement: Toward a shared future? *Diversity & Democracy, 19*(3). Retrieved from https://www.aacu.org/diversitydemocracy/2016/summer/mcbride

Ogbor, J. O. (2000). Mythicizing and reification in entrepreneurial discourse: Ideology-critique of entrepreneurial studies. *Journal of Management Studies, 37*(5), 605–635.

O'Meara, K., & Rice, R. E. (2005). *Faculty priorities reconsidered: Rewarding multiple forms of scholarship*. San Francisco, CA: Jossey-Bass.

Phills, J. A., Deiglmeier, K., & Miller, D. T. (2008, Fall). Rediscovering social innovation. *Stanford Social Innovation Review*. Retrieved from https://ssir.org/articles/entry/rediscovering_social_innovation

Saltmarsh, J. (2005). The civic promise of service learning. *Liberal Education, 91*(2), 50–55.

Saltmarsh, J., & Hartley, M. (Eds.). (2011). *To serve a larger purpose: Engagement for democracy and the transformation of higher education*. Philadelphia, PA: Temple University Press.

Saltmarsh, J., Hartley, M., & Clayton, P. (2009). *Democratic Engagement White Paper*. Boston, MA: New England Resource Center for Higher Education.

Saltmarsh, J., & Johnson, M. B. (2018). *The elective Carnegie Community Engagement Classification*. Boston, MA: Campus Compact.

Scobey, D. (2010). Across: Heterogeneity of civic education. In M. B. Smith, R. S. Nowacek, & J. L. Bernstein (Eds.), *Citizenship across the curriculum* (pp. 185–198). Bloomington: Indiana University Press.

Scobey, D. (2015, October 25). *Social innovation and civic engagement: Sibling rivals or kissing cousins?* Address delivered at Think Tank on Social Innovation and Civic Engagement in Higher Education, Washington University, St. Louis, MO.

Sharma, J. (2016, September 19). A neoliberal takeover of social entrepreneurship? *Stanford Social Innovation Review*. Retrieved from https://ssir.org/articles/entry/a_neoliberal_takeover_of_social_entrepreneurship

Sharma, J. (2017, October 18). Avoiding the neoliberal trap in social entrepreneurship. *Stanford Social Innovation Review*. Retrieved from https://ssir.org/articles/entry/avoiding_the_neoliberal_trap_in_social_entrepreneurship

Slaughter, S., & Rhoades, G. (2000). *Academic capitalism and the new economy*. Princeton, NJ: Princeton University Press.

Sturm, S., Eatman, T., Saltmarsh, J., & Bush, A. (2011). Full participation: Building the architecture for diversity and community engagement in higher education. *Imagining America, 17*, 24.

Thomas, N. (2011). *Educating for deliberative democracy: New directions for higher education* (Vol. 152). San Francisco, CA: Jossey-Bass.

Weiskopf, R., & Steyaert, C. (2009). Metamorphoses in entrepreneurship studies: Towards an affirmative politics of entrepreneuring. In D. Hjorth & C. Steyaert (Eds.), *The politics and aesthetics of entrepreneurship* (pp. 183–201). Cheltenham UK: Edward Elgar.

Chapter Eight

REALIZING HIGHER EDUCATION'S DEMOCRATIC PROMISE

The Next Chapter for Civic Engagement and Social Innovation

Amanda Moore McBride and Eric Mlyn

The contributors to this book have a deep and abiding commitment to higher education and the ways it can contribute to social change. They describe efforts on their campuses to educate future leaders and changemakers, who work for a more just world; they identify over-arching themes that transcend unique campus cultures and initiatives; and they make clear that the highest potential of both the civic engagement and social innovation movements has yet to be achieved. The resounding conclusion is that the democratic goals of higher education need to be made manifest in both movements—and that both approaches have fallen short. Our society and the pursuit of social change—indeed, the very health of our democracy—will benefit from the crucial and fundamental enhancement of this work.

We offer a summary of the themes across this book that pertain to the evolution and possible trajectory of the approaches. We muse about the democratic purpose of higher education overall and how our campuses might better realize this purpose through our civic engagement and social innovation efforts. We offer specific structural, programmatic, and pedagogical strategies for how we might improve these important approaches in higher education. And we seek to do this by focusing on the educational process and its impacts on individuals and, collectively, on society.

Perhaps at the most basic and general level, both approaches believe that universities can and should and do attempt to make the world a better place. Though this is not a particularly controversial comment today, there are critics such as Stanley Fish (2008) who feel strongly, to paraphrase the title of his book, that university faculty and staff should "save the world on their own time." Of course, there are some fields in the academy that are more or less prone to be involved in the mission to make the world a better place. And, at a similar level of generality, the contributors to this volume agree that both civic engagement and social innovation as they presently find themselves lack a fundamental democratic commitment. Caryn McTighe Musil adds, related to this point, that both also fail to take seriously the important democratic commitments that come with taking diversity seriously. Mathew Johnson and colleagues try to remedy this flaw by suggesting trajectories that would help us to achieve a better version of these approaches with the aspiration of creating democratic civic engagement and democratic social innovation, both with an increased focus on reciprocity with communities. These authors are not the first to decry the loss of our democratic purpose, but given the overall lack of progress toward this goal, we see this as a very important reminder. As editors of this volume, we find ourselves moved by the democratic consensus that has emerged within it.

The Evolution of Movements

Through what has been an honest and openly self-critical approach, higher education is improving on its pedagogies that are intended to contribute to social change. The chapters in this book support this view. We can trace the civic engagement movement from its roots in service and charitable patronage to service-learning that emphasized the learning more than the service to the emergence and prioritization of mutual, reciprocal community partnerships in teaching and learning. Increased attention to the role of the community and the assessment of outcomes for both students and the communities with which they engage have been central to the evolution of the field. The field has also become constructively self-critical, thankfully not to the point of paralysis but instead in a way that has aided us in improving our practices and thus better designing civic engagement to not only help our students learn but also provide tangible benefits to our community.

The social innovation movement, while more nascent, is also improving its goals and methods—from a flash focus on the new and novel entrepreneur to innovation as a process to now an emphasis on applicability and likelihood of success, even including the role that community responsiveness plays in this approach. Fruitful dialogue and overlap between civic engagement and social innovation scholars and higher education programs and offices—as is evidenced in this volume—are helping share lessons learned from the older civic engagement movement to the newer approaches that rely on social innovation. Furthermore, by looking more deeply into the origins of the social innovation and entrepreneurship approach—as, for example, David Scobey does with his insightful discussion of Muhammad Yunus—we can see that community voice and needs have sometimes been important for this approach. And we expect this trend to continue as volumes such as this and gatherings that bring practitioners and scholars from both fields together share best practices and lessons learned. Importantly, Ashoka U, the leading national and international organization promoting higher education and social entrepreneurship, has been commendably open to critique and lessons learned as well as very open to involvement from the more traditional civic engagement community. We hope and expect this to continue as well.

Moving Civic Engagement and Social Innovation Forward

In view of the insights offered throughout this book, we contend that we need a reinvigoration of purpose and even a new organizing framework for higher education's approach to social change. We think that the purpose may rest in the democratic promise of higher education, and that we should embrace our role as anchor institutions in the full sense—across social, economic, cultural, and political dimensions. Both movements may prioritize community engagement more than they have in the past, but more is needed here and to go one step further—to realize the democratic promise of higher education with a new focus on systems-level change and how we approach our engagement in our home communities and with those communities for which our university resources and intellectual assets can best be leveraged, wherever they may be. In this way, we organize our reflections from vision to structure to strategies.

Vision: The Democratic Promise

Much has been said about the democratic purpose of higher education—from Thomas Jefferson; *Higher Education for American Democracy*, the report commissioned by President Harry Truman (President's Commission on Higher Education, 1947); and more recent utterances from *A Crucible Moment: College Learning and Democracy's Future* (National Task Force on Civic Learning and Democratic Engagement, 2012). Further, for those of you reading this chapter who have a role in higher education, take a look at the mission statement of your institution. No doubt that you will find reference to preparing citizens, leaders, people of purpose, or the like. Our predecessors have not been particularly clear on what exactly we have meant about the democratic purpose of higher education, other than a general but clear sense that higher education had an important role in building and defending democracy. Though more surely deserves to be said about this, the purpose relates in the most general way to educating the citizenry for democracy and to the fact that very specific curricular and cocurricular offerings can enhance students' democratic participation.

Here we draw on the seminal work *Educating for Democracy: Preparing Undergraduates for Responsible Political Engagement* (Colby, Beaumont, Ehrlich, & Corngold, 2007). This remains one of the clearest and most comprehensive looks at the public purpose of higher education, the goals of that purpose, and what kinds of practices promote citizenship and democratic engagement. Colby and colleagues urge, as others in the field have as well, that educating for democratic purposes should focus on student development in three areas:

1. *Political understanding*: This includes knowledge about political theories and how government works as well as important political and economic issues.
2. *Political skills*: This includes the capability to understand how to exercise political influence (e.g., deliberation and persuasion) and political action (e.g., voter registration and voting).
3. *Political motivation*: The authors point out that we know this is linked to political knowledge and rests on students seeing politics as relevant to their lives and that their political actions matter, that they have some sense of political efficacy.

While the aforementioned focus on the general developmental goals for educating for citizenship and democracy, we also want to take this analysis a step further by more clearly elucidating what democratic action can accomplish. Democratic action for social change demands the prioritization of marginalized voices. This is Caryn McTighe Musil's point regarding diversity, and it is important for us to keep in mind her apt observation that not everybody is equally able to be a changemaker, as is sometimes implied by the social innovation movement in higher education, and that the democratic promise is both process and outcome. To realize this promise means that we must teach how disparity is created and maintained, such that reduction of disparity and marginalization is an outcome of any social change efforts and thus a step toward strengthening of democracy.

Civic engagement approaches in higher education have largely failed on this front, prioritizing charity over change, while social innovation approaches have often stoked hubris and individualism over commonality and collectivism. The focus for democratic training, where it does exist, tends to be on the undergraduate student, though it should apply at all levels of learning—undergraduate, graduate, professional, and lifelong. It also has a place across the disciplines and professions, not just in those more directly considered social or political.

A focus on the democratic promise would mean that social outcomes of any effort are prioritized as much as or more than economic outcomes. This applies to not only social innovation efforts but also civic engagement. For example, in the name of international service-learning, many of our programs can actually displace local labor instead of being in service to it. Our colleagues have urged this in the development of "Fair Trade Learning" (Hartman, Morris-Paris, & Blache-Cohn, 2013). It also means that policy and political action would be prioritized when deciding how to take innovations that work to scale. Imagine student teams working to understand the components of social movements and how the public can be mobilized for action, and then planning for how a given innovation with proven results could find its way into local, state, or federal policies.

And a focus on the democratic promise here would underscore the fundamental role that all of the U.S. education system—K–12 and higher education—would play in educating an informed citizenry, a necessary component of nearly all conceptions of a strong democracy. At the time of this writing, proposals for free public education have proliferated. And though these bold but increasingly common initiatives are often justified in terms of job readiness or workforce development, there can be no doubt that one of the fundamental necessities of a strong democracy is an educated citizenry. Making higher education more accessible would surely go a long way toward creating this essential educated citizenry.

Structure: Anchor Institution as an Organizing Framework

The anchor institution framework can be a comprehensive organizing device for all of a university's local efforts, advancing basic democratic tenets across the range of social, economic, cultural, and political efforts. As a framework, it has implications for the academic as well as the operational enterprise. Hartley and his colleagues make it clear that at a very fundamental level the anchor institution framework, with its focus on the *institution's* most immediate locale, cannot avoid programs and approaches that are deeply embedded in democratic aspirations and sensibilities. The framework suggests that our conceptions of democracy are rooted in the local, something that can be elusive for some sectors of American higher education that aspire to have larger global profiles. The framework also means that the institution must be up front and honest about its power and privilege and also own what it uniquely brings to the community and any community partnership. Approaching community partnership with this ethos is still not the norm in higher education.

While this ethos must embody this framework for maximum effectiveness, so must a correspondingly mission-driven structure. Both civic engagement and social innovation efforts may aim to engage community but often do it in isolation from one another—with the same organization, neighborhood, or population being approached by a university's civic engagement center as well as its social innovation center and individual faculty and students in between. The respective movements could be advanced further if there was a defined entity or organizing device for approaching and collaborating with the community. In this way, we are actually saying that to truly have the community drive this work, to truly put marginalized voices at the center means that we have to change the way universities structure their interface with community. The onus should be on us to reduce the opportunity and transaction costs for collaborating with higher education. If we are just wielding our weight with community or encouraging (or allowing) students' privilege in their interface with community, then we will not realize our democratic promise; community is just a pawn in the learning and the self-service of our students. Further, we will not realize the promise if our community partners can serve as laboratories for our students and faculty but at a most basic level cannot park on our campuses or use our libraries.

Here we wonder if our institutions might adopt the approach used by cities across the United States, namely that citizens are offered one phone number to access all city services. What if our institutions did the same for our proximate communities, and they could reach out to us to access our resources and expertise? And then, rather than reaching out to communities with an approach that sits in the "innovation hub" instead of the "civic engagement office," we suggest looking at community issues holistically and drawing on the part(s) of the university that together decide how best to use community and university assets to address community needs.

Strategies: Pedagogy and Content

Community engagement is the lynchpin of effectiveness for civic engagement and social innovation initiatives, courses, processes, and outcomes. It is the method by which we pursue our democratic process—through an anchor institution structure and through the pedagogy of our classrooms. As far as community engagement is concerned, civic engagement and social innovation efforts could better teach and model this method, and it has become clear to us in editing this volume that there is nothing inherently antidemocratic about either movement. The following recommendations apply to both.

Both faculty and staff interface with our students as undergraduate and graduate students' civic engagement and social innovation activities span the curricular and cocurricular spaces. As a matter of living our values, the faculty and staff should be trained themselves in the democratic promise of higher education and how then to translate it into their responsibilities. This means whether they are participating in a service-learning course or a hackathon, we would encourage our students to examine power and privilege in all aspects of the community engagement process. Examples of actualizing the democratic promise in community engagement include the following:

- Teaching the community engagement partnership process with a focus on inclusion of marginalized and affected populations.
- Teaching how to engage community in problem definition, such as through participatory action research approaches and group model building.
- Engaging community partners and community members in the coeducational process as experts.
- Weighing students' experiences and immersion with the voices of the community partners and assessing the degree to which this was achieved for all involved, holding us accountable; this includes involving community members in all aspects of the engagement process.

- Ensuring that students do not see communities and people as merely problems to be solved but as replete with strengths, resources, and potential, which if leveraged will maximize the success of any effort.

We do our students, our community, and our society a disservice when we oversimplify social issues. Social change requires systems-level change, and changing systems requires knowledge of and the skills to work with those systems. We think that social change has at its core an understanding of the policy process and politics. It is clear to us through our work in this field that this has been missing from many of higher education's approaches to social change. Though this is not the place to reflect extensively on why this might be the case, it is no doubt at least partially linked to the pressures on universities to appear to be nonpartisan and apolitical; however, higher education's shirking of responsibility means that system-level change will remain elusive. Our students' and institutions' efforts will continue to largely focus on private (nonprofit and corporate) responses to public issues, which government may be more uniquely positioned to address. If we leave this unquestioned, we do so at the peril of the vitality of our democracy.

Imagining again the pedagogical process in both curricular and cocurricular civic engagement and social innovation spaces on our campuses, we need to explore and educate on the role of local, state, and federal government policies in the social issues our students aim to address. More and more students arrive on our campuses unable to explain how a bill becomes law, which means that we must teach the policy process and the role of citizen action in the policy process. Otherwise, our students' imaginations will not be able to envision social change through all the levers possible. This also means that social movements, mobilization, and all the means of drawing forth citizen action and impact must be known. Teaching about social change through the policy process does not have to be done in the abstract. Case study examples will captivate students' imaginations, while also incentivizing the skeptics among them as to a proper role of government. Perhaps looking at what started as innovations with a social purpose—successes such as Teach for America and City Year that in order to be sustained and scaled were able to secure government funding through political and policy processes at both the state and federal levels—can help illustrate how social innovation must ultimately contend with political processes necessary for scaling.

Learning how to scale social change through policy has important intersections between civic engagement and social innovation. Students of both inclinations can work together to help communities scale evidence-based innovations through policy by analyzing options, funding mechanisms, and potential intended and unintended consequences. Students can also research community interests and organizations that have a stake in the potential policy, along with those legislative and congressional leaders who are mostly likely to sponsor and support the legislation.

In addition to the importance of scale as a way to combine democratic engagement with innovation, civic tech is one area that we find particularly exciting and wonderfully connects social innovation and democratic engagement. Civic tech is in its most basic form the use of technology to enhance democratic participation by creating web- or app-based platforms to access what is already publicly available data. These kinds of services, often free, have proliferated over the last decade and have great promise to better connect our students and citizens more generally to traditional mechanisms of political participation through innovative uses of technology. Many have the remarkable potential to enhance democratic engagement by providing easy ways for users to access data that already exists in the public sphere, whether that be congressional voting records, voter rolls, or more general electoral information. And although higher education does not have a monopoly on the promulgation of these services, it certainly can be a place where students are exposed to the great potential of civic tech. It is also a place where the increasingly popular computer science major on many of our campuses can enhance democratic engagement.

Here are a few prominent and exciting examples:

- TurboVote (2019): Helps users register to vote, apply for absentee ballots, and know the dates and locations for voting.
- VoteWithMe (2019): A mobile app that syncs a user's address book to public voter rolls and tells you who has voted, allowing the user to contact friends and family to urge them to vote.
- Countable (2019): Allows the user to read summaries of legislation, helps citizens know who their legislator is and communicate their opinions on bills, and then provides follow-up on how representatives voted on bills.

These examples demonstrate the STEM disciplines in service to community and democracy. We do not yet have good evidence of the impact of these services on democratic participation, but we want to urge our colleagues in public policy, political science, and computer science to collaborate to help meld what we know about democratic behavior with technological innovation as a way to help promote the democratic promise of higher education.

The Future

To be sure, some campuses are already doing what we recommend. A few select examples are evidenced in this book. However, we all have a way to go in realizing higher education's democratic promise through the methods we use and the substance we teach. It is clear that we and the contributors to this volume are surely not the first to call for this democratic reinvigoration, so we need to fully explore the real obstacles to achieving this long-term vision. These recommendations may move us a few more steps toward effective development of individuals who pursue social change and the bolstering of the democratic purpose of American higher education. Implementation of these recommendations, however, does not necessarily prepare our students for the world of the future. We think it is worth considering possible future versions of society as well as higher education that may impact how social change is pursued and achieved.

How society is organized is changing. The Scottish Enlightenment's defined functions of the public, private, and citizenry sectors are blurring. Eventually, there may be few tax-code lines between the corporate and social sectors. The triple bottom line of people, profits, and the planet may become the focus of the corporate and social sectors alike—and frankly the youth across our campuses are demanding this focus. There may be a future where for-profit corporations are held to a triple bottom line and so are nonprofits, foundations, B Corps, L3Cs, and on and on. With the functional blurring comes a direct challenge to our disciplinary homes and boundaries, such as public policy and political science, business and economics, and social work and sociology. It also challenges what we teach and to whom and for what ends. The rise in interdisciplinary innovation and entrepreneurial centers and institutes supports this shift, yet many of them do not have credit-bearing authority or assume a posture to train for social change across the tools of each sector. This will be needed if social efforts are increasingly pursued and supported through for-profit means.

Higher education's value proposition is under siege and is the ultimate disruptor for the industry. Our unique value and to whom and for what price is changing. Online graduate and professional education is one example. As the locus of place and proximity shifts from centralized to decentralized and diffused, our approach and pedagogy will need to change. For example, several contributors to this volume made the argument that to realize an anchor institution approach means to focus locally, assuming the "main campus" as the anchor. However, online education has radically shifted how our institutions show up in communities across the country. Moreover, not having students physically present in one place where we can teach and model the skills of community engagement may or may not compromise their democratic learning, but it is a possibility worth tracking and is a challenge to develop new pedagogies.

After diving deeply into the worlds of civic engagement and social innovation and engaging the arguments of our coauthors, we come away with a new understanding of how these approaches relate to each other. Each has had enough cross-pollination between them that, on the important issues of democratic underpinnings and community engagement, we cannot necessarily differentiate these approaches, whether they are in the civic engagement or social innovation schools of thought.

Moving forward, we urge our higher education colleagues to examine each particular approach according to how much it does all the things that we think are important for any approach to social change. Notwithstanding the important and fascinating findings of Clifford and colleagues in chapter 4 of this volume, we are witnessing a time of convergence. Perhaps the best example of this in this book is the history of the University of San Diego as an anchor institution, helping to moderate the "everybody-a-changemaker" charge that is such an important part of the social innovation movement. This is a wonderful case study and metaphor for how dialogue among these approaches can lead to better university-wide structures, collaboration, and pedagogy among these approaches. And as we hope this volume illustrates, the achievement of this dialogue and collaboration is more than an academic exercise. The strength of our democracy rests on this shared ground.

References

Colby, A., Beaumont, E., Ehrlich, T., & Corngold, J. (2007). *Educating for democracy: Preparing undergraduates for responsible political engagement.* San Francisco, CA: Jossey-Bass.

Countable. (2019). *Make your voice heard.* Retrieved from https://www.countable.us/

Fish, S. (2008). *Save the world on your own time.* New York, NY: Oxford University Press.

Hartman, E., Morris-Paris, C., & Blache-Cohn, B. (2012). Tourism and transparency: Navigating ethical risks in voluntourism with fair trade learning. *Africa Insight*, 42(2), 157-168.

National Task Force on Civic Learning and Democratic Engagement. (2012). *A crucible moment: College learning and democracy's future*. Washington, DC: Association of American Colleges & Universities.

President's Commission on Higher Education. (1947). *Higher education for American democracy, Vol. I, Establishing the goals*. Washington, DC: Government Printing Office.

TurboVote. (2019). *TurboVote*. Retrieved from https://turbovote.org/

VoteWithMe. (2019). *VoteWithMe*. Retrieved from https://votewithme.us/

CONTRIBUTORS

Amy Anderson is a faculty consultant for Duke Service-Learning at Duke University, where she also serves as an assistant professor of the practice in the program in education. Threads that connect her work include exploration of how K–12 and higher education can produce, reproduce, and resist conditions that limit participation, engagement, and equity for all students and a belief in the responsibility of higher education to facilitate integration of students' coherent pathways through college, bringing curricular and cocurricular experiences into generative conversation with each other.

Joan Clifford is assistant professor of the practice in Spanish in the Department of Romance Studies at Duke University and is affiliate faculty in the Duke Global Health Institute. Within Duke Service-Learning she supports faculty across the disciplines and as director of the Community-Based Language Initiative works closely with world language faculty. Her research interests include best practices in community engagement, community-based language learning, and intercultural communicative competence.

Dane Emmerling is a PhD student in the health behavior department of Gillings School of Global Public Health at the University of North Carolina at Chapel Hill. He specializes in critical consciousness–raising interventions, community engagement, and cocurricular learning and assessment.

Kevin Guerrieri is an associate professor in the Department of Languages, Cultures and Literatures and a faculty liaison in the Mulvaney Center for Community, Awareness and Social Action at the University of San Diego. His teaching and research interests include Latin American literature and culture, human rights and cultural production, and the scholarship of engagement.

Ira Harkavy is associate vice president and founding director of the Barbara and Edward Netter Center for Community Partnerships at the

University of Pennsylvania. Harkavy has written and lectured widely on the history and current practice of urban university-community-school partnerships and the democratic and civic missions of higher education. Among his most recent books is *Knowledge for Social Change: Bacon, Dewey, and the Revolutionary Transformation of Research Universities in the Twenty-First Century* (Temple University Press, 2017; coauthored with Lee Benson, John Puckett, Matthew Hartley, Rita A. Hodges, Francis E. Johnston, and Joann Weeks).

Matthew Hartley serves as associate dean in the Graduate School of Education and professor of education at the University of Pennsylvania. Hartley's areas of expertise include academic governance and leadership in higher education, institutional mission, civic engagement and the democratic purposes of higher education, and higher education reform. He serves on the editorial boards of *The Review of Higher Education* and the *Journal of Higher Education Engagement and Outreach.*

Rita A. Hodges is assistant director of the Barbara and Edward Netter Center for Community Partnerships at the University of Pennsylvania. Hodges supports all aspects of the center's mission and operations to improve the quality of life in the community while simultaneously advancing research, teaching, learning, and service at the university. Her writing and doctoral research have focused on the democratic engagement of colleges and universities as anchor institutions.

Mathew B. Johnson is executive director of the Howard R. Swearer Center and associate dean of engaged scholarship at Brown University. He also codirects the Carnegie Community Engagement Classification and its International Research Project on behalf of the Carnegie Foundation for the Advancement of Teaching and is the cofounder and codirector of the National Assessment of Service and Community Engagement.

prabhdeep singh kehal is a PhD candidate in sociology at Brown University and a graduate fellow in community-engaged scholarship at the Howard R. Swearer Center. The center's research explores how scholars define and recognize the nature of racialized organizations and what implications arise for social change once scholars account for an organization's racialization. Its projects consider how merit has been historically constructed within higher education by exploring the relationship among slavery, colonialism, faculty, and higher education.

Judith Liu is a professor of sociology and a faculty liaison in the Mulvaney Center for Community, Awareness and Social Action. She has written a number of articles on service-learning and community engagement pedagogy.

David Malone is professor of the practice of education at Duke University and faculty director of the Office of Service-Learning. His scholarly interests include educational psychology, school psychology, student-centered approaches to teaching and learning, experiential learning, critical service-learning, and innovative educational approaches in higher education.

Amanda Moore McBride is the Morris Endowed Dean and a professor at the Graduate School of Social Work at the University of Denver and adviser to the university's innovation and entrepreneurship initiative, Project X-ITE. Prior to 2016, McBride was the Bettie Bofinger Brown associate professor at the George Warren Brown School of Social Work and the founding executive director of the Gephardt Institute for Civic and Community Engagement, Washington University, in St. Louis.

Eric Mlyn is a distinguished faculty fellow at the Kenan Institute for Ethics and a lecturer at the Sanford School of Public Policy at Duke University. He is the founding director of DukeEngage and led that program until July 2019.

Caryn McTighe Musil is a senior scholar and director of civic learning and democracy initiatives at the Association of American Colleges & Universities.

Chris Nayve serves as assistant provost for community engagement at the University of San Diego (USD). He also serves as director for the Mulvaney Center for Community, Awareness and Social Action and is an adviser to USD's Changemaker Hub. He was the 2016 winner of the Richard E. Cone Award for Excellence and Leadership in Cultivating Community Partnerships in Higher Education.

Juan Carlos Rivas is assistant director of the Changemaker Hub at the University of San Diego. He is currently in his fourth year of the Leadership Studies doctoral program and a faculty member of the RISE Urban Leadership Fellow Program.

David Scobey is currently director of Bringing Theory to Practice, a national initiative based in Washington DC, that works to advance holistic, engaged college learning through innovative practice, research, and institutional change. A cultural historian and American studies scholar, he taught at Brandeis University, the University of Michigan, and Bates College and served as a dean at The New School. For 20 years, he has been a leading advocate of civic engagement in higher education; undergraduate reform; and the needs of adult, nontraditional college students.

Sandra Sgoutas-Emch is a professor in the Department of Psychological Sciences and director of the Center for Educational Excellence at the University of San Diego. She received a faculty fellowship from the California Campus Compact–Carnegie Foundation for service-learning for political engagement and was a national finalist for the Thomas Ehrlich Civically Engaged Faculty Award for civic engagement and the public good by Campus Compact in 2015.

Joann Weeks is an associate director of the Barbara and Edward Netter Center for Community Partnerships at the University of Pennsylvania, focusing on its regional, national, and international programs. Weeks directs the national adaptation of the Netter Center's university-assisted community school program, as well as its training and technical assistance activities, including the university-assisted community schools network.

Evan Widney is a research analyst in the Office of Assessment at Duke University. His work focuses on developing and supporting cultures of evidence and inquiry within academic communities, with an emphasis on program evaluation and the assessment of student learning outcomes.

Mike Williams is an associate professor of political science and international relations and director of the Changemaker Hub at the University of San Diego. He specializes in democratization, civil society, and state-building in sub-Saharan Africa and, more specifically, South Africa.

Cadence Willse is a postdoctoral research fellow at the Center for Philanthropy and Civil Society at Stanford University. She received her PhD in political science at Brown University, where she was a graduate fellow in community-engaged scholarship at the Howard R. Swearer Center. Willse's research focuses on civic advocacy in American politics, and her dissertation addresses the rapid increase in philanthropic-based advocacy in public schools.

Index

The Community Engagement Professional's Guidebook

A Companion to The Community Engagement Professional in Higher Education

By Lina D. Dostilio and Marshall Welch

This guidebook offers a rich and deep dive into the practice of higher education community engagement, breaking down the essential competencies that are inherent in a professional's work. From leading campaigns to build civic engagement curriculum on campus, to mentoring faculty research, to managing staff who support community engagement units, Dostilio and Welch tackle the full breadth of the community engagement professional's (CEP) work. The book includes interactive moments that call for personal reflection on one's knowledge, skills, commitments, and ongoing experiences as a CEP, creating a powerful and engaging toolkit that should be considered essential for any person doing community and civic engagement work on and off campus.

Also available from Campus Compact

The Craft of Community-Engaged Teaching and Learning

A Guide for Faculty Development

By Marshall Welch and Star Plaxton-Moore

"*The Craft of Community-Engaged Teaching and Learning* is a competency-based blueprint for professional growth in engaged teaching and learning. . . . This book and its accompanying workbook will be my go-to guide for my work to develop faculty capacity—not just to teach community-engaged courses, but to become a community-engaged scholar and master of the craft of engaged teaching and learning."—***Cathy Jordan***, *Professor of Pediatrics and Extension Specialist, University of Minnesota*

"Drawing on the most recent literature in the field and critical theory, as well as the knowledge of two seasoned practitioners, this book will help build faculty capacity for high-quality community-engaged teaching and learning whether one is just starting to hone their pedagogical craft or seeking to deepen their practice."—***John Saltmarsh***, *Professor of Higher Education; University of Massachusetts, Boston*

Written in a conversational voice, this unique book provides detailed counsel on how to advance one's craft as a community-engaged scholar, from the design of community-engaged courses to preparing for tenure and promotion. A range of interactive activities are interspersed throughout the chapters, and an accompanying interactive workbook can be downloaded from the Campus Compact website. Both this book and the workbook can be used by individual practitioners or within a learning community.

(Continues on preceding page)